PRAISE FOR *RUNNING HOME*

"Alisha Perkins has gone to dark places, haunted by demons that threatened her very existence. But she chose to fight back, and found solace and freedom through running. Hers is a story of triumph over tragedy, and in her book she speaks honestly and openly about crawling from the depths to find the light."

—Dean Karnazes, ultramarathoner and *New York Times* best-selling author

"It's as authentic a story as I've ever read. There is nothing quite so endearing as honesty. . . . Reading it felt like a long walk with an old friend."

—Kevin Slowey, former MLB pitcher and current special assistant, MLB Players Association

"Want to read something honest and bold? The reason I enjoyed this book so much was because I know it is true. Alisha is brave enough to share thoughts and experiences that most of us wouldn't be willing to say out loud."

—Bekah Metzdorff, owner of Mill City Running

"*Running Home* is the story of two kinds of races. One is run with a good pair of Nikes and the other with the heart. Alisha inspires with her very personal and candid story about becoming a runner and about her resilient determination to cope with chronic anxiety. Her story will make you want to take up running, and it will also give you hope for whatever inherent struggles you may be facing."

—Debbie Scheide, LMFT

"Alisha's perspective is honest, vulnerable, and inspirational. It offers hope when one needs it most."

—Virginia Achman, executive director, Twin Cities in Motion

"I loved reading this book. Alisha opens herself up in a way most of us would only do on a run with a girlfriend or a training partner. Sharing her secrets, passions, fears, setbacks, and achievements made me feel like I was running the roads with her and about to get after life! Thanks for letting us take a sneak peek of the life of wife, mommy, and runner Alisha Perkins."

—Carrie Tollefson, US Olympic runner

"Anxiety and other forms of mental illness are mostly untalked-about subjects in this country. . . . Credit to Alisha for opening up about her struggles, and for pulling back the curtain on a hobby—running—that has helped guide her through. Honest, insightful, funny, and relatable."

—Phil Mackey, ESPN radio host

"*Running Home* is artfully woven together with strands of an uplifting sports story, a passionate love story, a story of overcoming, and a remarkably candid story of the reality of living with mental illness. What makes this book so powerful is that it is an unfiltered *true* story, and Alisha Perkins's voice is so genuine that you can't help but relate. *Running Home* has perfect timing—entering a national climate that is finally warming to the notion of breaking the stigma on anxiety and other mental illnesses. Perkins wears so many 'hats'— Twins wife, mother, runner, fighter, writer, Minnesotan, philanthropist, believer . . . no matter who you are and what 'hats' you may wear, I think we all can gain something from reading her story."

—Heather Kampf, Team USA MN, Asics Elite athlete

"A fun and lighthearted read that just may inspire you to lace up those boots and run home. Much appreciation for her honesty! Every baseball wife has their story, and this is hers, loud and proud!"

—Renee Dozier, wife of MLB player Brian Dozier

"This book is amazing. It helped me realize why I started to run, why I run now, and why I feel the need to run. Alisha's style is very humble, authentic, and inspirational. She shares her heartaches, triumphs, pain, and pleasure. Alisha's description of her ongoing bout with anxiety will open the eyes to those that battle the same thing and help them realize they are not the only ones feeling like this. She is very brave to share details regarding the need to overbook to prevent downtime, and about her getting worn out and shutting down. Luckily for her and the reader, running gave Alisha her voice back. She now enjoys that downtime when she doesn't have to think or talk. Her message will inspire others to know that there is nothing to hide. . . . This book will be eye-opening for those that currently run and hopefully motivate others to start."

—Danny McCormack, Nike Baseball

"Sometimes we use running as a means of escape. Alisha teaches us it may actually be the best way to confront our most brutal burdens. This poignant, funny, and unapologetically raw examination of life in the public eye helps us reexamine why we spend so much energy trying to be what others think we should be, instead of just finding our own stride and breaking out from the pack. A truly inspiring read!"

—Eric Perkins, KARE 11 anchor

"What I love about running—as much as the endorphin high—is the camaraderie among running partners, and as often happens, a baring of the soul at a shared pace. And that's what Alisha Perkins offers in *Running Home*. She shows us her vulnerability, all while doing something that makes her feel strong."

—Kara Douglass Thom, author of *Go! Go! Sports Girls* children's book series and coauthor of *Hot (Sweaty) Mamas: Five Secrets to Life as a Fit Mom*

"You feel as though you are running alongside Alisha as she takes you on her candid journey. She illustrates how running can be so much more than a race to the finish line. It is what you learn about yourself along the way that can matter most."

—Maddie Mauer, wife of MLB player Joe Mauer

"Alisha Perkins's ruminations on the beauty of life, the perils of anxiety, and the comfort of family breathe wisdom amid humor and solemnity. This is a brave book, and like its author, it takes off running and promises never to slow down."

—Jeff Passan, author of *The Arm*

"*Running Home* is a brutally honest and engrossing story about a woman's struggles with clinical anxiety and how she overcomes challenges through grit, determination, and, sometimes, running. Perkins's openness and wit present her story in an entertaining and accessible manner. Her life is extraordinary, but her humble and frank approach makes her struggle and story relevant for all too many of us living in and dealing with first-world issues in twenty-first-century America."

—Karl Hoagland, publisher of *Ultrarunning Magazine*

"A refreshingly honest tale about the power of the mind and the body. Anxiety is a mental illness with no start line or finish line, but Perkins shows us that running is her clearest path to health."

—Michael Rand, *Minneapolis Star-Tribune* Digital Sports Editor

"A raw and honest account of her journey from a neophyte runner to a seasoned veteran. Athletes of all levels will be able to relate to Alisha Perkins's struggles and successes in *Running Home*. A must-read for runners seeking to be inspired."

—Jeff Metzdorff, owner of Mill City Running

"Alisha Perkins's *Running Home* is a beautiful book that, on the surface, is about running, but is actually about so much more. It is about dealing with anxiety, finding balance in life, and remembering to run toward something and not away from anything. It will inspire you and, perhaps, even get you to pick up your old running shoes and start again."

—Joe Posnanski, *New York Times* bestselling author and national columnist for NBC Sports

Running Home

Running Home

Big-League Wife, Small-Town Story

Foreword by Three-Time MLB All-Star Glen Perkins

Alisha Perkins

NORTH LOOP BOOKS | MINNEAPOLIS, MN

North Loop Books
322 First Avenue N, 5th floor
Minneapolis, MN 55401
612.455.2294
www.NorthLoopBooks.com

ISBN-13: 978-1-63505-105-6
LCCN: 2016902788

All photos courtesy of the author.

Distributed by Itasca Books

Book Design by B. Cook

Printed in the United States of America

DEDICATED TO:

Lover
The first man who chose to love all of me,
in spite of me.

Cakes
The first girl to steal my heart.

Beanie
The last piece of our family puzzle
that made us feel whole.

CONTENTS

FOREWORD

When I sat down to write this, I thought to myself, "This should be easy. Alisha just wrote how many thousands of words. I can charm and BS my way through a thousand, no problem."

That was five months ago, in July.

So here I am in December, finally getting to this foreword. I think that is the biggest difference between me and her. Alisha, as she explains so well in the chapters that follow, is a consummate type A. I am somewhere off in the distance, past a type B.

When we met in college I was, and still am, a dumb jock. I was so smitten by her that I took classes just to be able to spend time with her. Education was secondary to me. Heck, I guess it was even tertiary. After baseball, then chasing her around, I found time for school, albeit only to follow her around like a dog wagging its tail with its tongue hanging out. Outside of her natural beauty, I was attracted to her drive and determination. She gave everything in her life 110 percent. There was no letting off the throttle. It was something I loved about her, and something that I hoped would rub off on me. She was the anti-me.

Now let's fast-forward a few years. We were at spring training. I don't remember the year (again, I'm a type B). Anyways, Alisha decides one day she is going to go for a run. She spends about twenty-six hours a day with our kids, and was looking for something to get her out of the house. Now, I know she talks about her first run in this book, but this is my foreword and I'm going to tell this story from my perspective.

So she leaves the house to go running. Her runs at this point consisted of what the runs of most mothers with two kids consist of—a mile here, two miles there. She says on her way out, "Be back in a bit," so I'm thinking, "This can't be too tough. The girls and I will play for a few minutes, and then she'll be back home to give me a hand. Twenty minutes ain't bad . . . I've got this."

After an hour I started to get a little worried. She never was gone for this long, and I was trying to entertain two toddlers. I needed help!

When she got back I asked what the hell had happened to her. Maybe she had to stopped to take a poop—as you'll soon learn, she sometimes does that when she runs. Maybe she ran a little and then started walking just to have some free time.

Nope, she started running and—much like Forrest Gump—just kept running until she got tired. She went something like five miles. She got the runner's high that day. A runner was born.

Over the first few years of our marriage Alisha tried out different hobbies and side businesses to try to carve out her own identity. When she started running, she almost by accident created an identity for herself she never thought possible. She would run, I would watch the kids. When she needed some free time she would run. When she was crabby I would tell her to go run. It was a match made in heaven—Alisha and running. I was beyond proud of her for finding something that she could relate to and that was "hers."

As time went on, her runs got longer and longer. Six miles, eight miles, Goldy's 10 Mile, half marathons, full marathons. Running became her thing. It's who she is. She didn't have to be "Glen Perkins's wife." She became "Alisha Perkins: runner."

Somewhere along the line she decided to start a blog, writing about her runs and offering self-help tips and inspirational quotes. Never did I—or Alisha, for that matter—think this would culminate into her writing a book. But here we are. Pages and pages of thousands and thousands of words. All from her heart.

She's put so much blood, sweat, and tears into running. Multiply that by 100, and that's what she has put into this book. For a shy, private, and anxious girl to share her thoughts and feelings with the world takes more strength and courage than anything I have ever done on a pitcher's mound.

Enjoy this book as I know you will. There is something for everyone in here. The runner, the runner's husband, wife, girlfriend, boyfriend. The person struggling with anxiety, or the partner of someone struggling with anxiety. Even the dumb jock husband who's scared to watch two toddlers by himself.

In the end, it's the story of a beautiful girl navigating life, a girl who continues to amaze me every day with her selflessness and grace, and whom I love with all my heart.

—Glen Perkins, three-time MLB All-Star

...

PROLOGUE

Your chest is tightening, breath shortening, mind racing, heart pounding. Gun to your back—you are being controlled by something else. You are out of your own mind, out of your body. Listening to what you are being told to do, what to think, your body responds to every heightened emotion. You lose your mind, your clarity, your overall thought process. Your adrenaline skyrockets and yet your body freezes. Your mind is racing and all you want is peace. You panic, you go blank. You have three options: you succumb, you fight, or you *RUN*.

Anxiety is a funny thing, one of those sneaky diseases you think you can control. In the beginning it seems to be situational and control-lable, but over time, or sometimes all at once, it changes, becoming something else entirely. It becomes this monster that can take over your life, change your every thought, and breed fear and stress.

When was it that I first discovered I had anxiety?

That is a tricky question. I am sure my anxiety has always been around in little ways, but for a long time I assumed this was just part of my type A personality. Moments throughout my childhood and young-adult life that should have been clues were written off as something I just needed to "get over." Feel the fear and do it anyway (as my therapist says) was the theme of my young days. I was a seemingly normal kid, willing to try new things, not shy, but there were moments, sure, where I gave more pause than others my age.

For me anxiety manifested after I had kids of my own. Maybe it was the hormone shift, maybe the newly felt responsibility, but something changed, and I spent years battling against something that I couldn't even name.

Everyone's story with anxiety is different, and no two are the same. For some it starts in childhood, others later in life; for some, anxiety is triggered by flying. As for me, I am totally fine with planes. Anxiety comes in all shapes and sizes, which is what makes it so difficult to understand and treat. What works for one person may not work for another.

There is a cloak of silence around mental illness in our society, largely because the generations before us didn't talk about it. They thought it made them different, and different wasn't good. It is also hard because there is no pen-and-paper way to prove you have it. There is no medical test that can show your neurotransmitters are off and therefore you are experiencing symptoms. I think it will be so helpful the day we can test people and be able to "prove" there is something going on. Right now it is just patients describing symptoms and doctors taking them at their word. For naysayers, this makes doctors look like pill pushers and sufferers seem like they just can't deal with everyday life.

Those of us living with anxiety know it is more than that, or at least we think we do, until someone doubts us. It is hard to explain anxiety to people who have never experienced it. I have spent countless hours trying to get Glen, my hubby, to empathize with me, but being the laid-back, type B guy that he is, all he can do is try to sympathize and encourage me to "run it out."

So we hide it, keep silent, and wait for the day that we no longer need to be ashamed of something beyond our control. For me, today is that day. I want to take that cloak of silence off, throw it down, and stomp the hell out of it. I want to tell you how I am living with this disorder and what has helped me cope. I am not a doctor or an expert on mental health. I am just an ordinary girl with an extraordinary husband, trying to outrun my issues while navigating life.

"I think I am going to throw up.
No, I know I am going to throw up.
Man, I hope I can at least park the car first."

–Me

. . .

MINNEAPOLIS MARATHON

June 1, 2013

I had gotten up at 5 a.m. because I could no longer sleep. I was awake in that "I can't miss my flight so I can't fully sleep" way. I tried my best to get ready, sitting on my hands until it was an appropriate time for me to leave the house. I felt ok. Nervous, but ok.

I got about ten minutes from the starting line and then it hit. I got jittery, anxious, and felt the bile rising in my throat. I can't do this, I thought. I am going to either puke or pass out before I even begin. I had never been so scared and panicked about a race before. I managed to park the car and take enough deep breaths to get to the porta-potty line, where I was sure I would toss my cookies.

I remember looking around wondering if anyone could tell that the color was draining from my face. I tried to remind myself to breathe, but being boxed into those portable toilets always makes me feel dizzy anyway; couple that with the fact that I was bordering on a panic attack, and I was in trouble.

Miraculously, I made it through my porta-potty experience unscathed and decided to go on a quick slow jog to calm my nerves. Apparently 26.2 wasn't far enough—I was going to add an extra half mile on top of that. Before I knew it I was lining up at the start, still trying to remember to breathe, and hoping that the extra adrenaline coursing through my veins would help me instead of making me faint.

The horn went off—they were no longer using guns since the Boston Marathon had gotten rid of them that year out of respect for the Sandy Hook Elementary victims in attendance—and I tried to ease my nerves, focus on the music, and break the race into manageable pieces. I knew I would see my parents at a few stops along the way, and they would have my kiddos with them in the cart behind their bike. I knew I would see Glen at the halfway point, my friends from the kids' school at mile 20, and my amazing cousin Bekah would join me at that point to run the last six miles with me.

I was feeling good and on the watch for anyone I might know, when around mile 2, my right knee started to throb.

I figured it was just a fluke and ran through it; there was no way I was going to give up months of training because my knee was acting up. I spent the next few miles getting lost in the music, scanning the crowd for familiar cheerers. I tried to disappear in the moment, let my feet do the work, and enjoy the first part of what I knew would be a long journey. By the time I saw Glen and my family at mile 13, my knee was barking pretty badly, but I was otherwise feeling good and making decent time.

Seeing my husband and kids gave me an adrenaline burst that helped me get my butt in gear and push through the pain. I got to see my parents and the kids again at mile 18, but Glen had to head to the baseball field and would have to rely on my parents' texts to find out how I was doing.

I really had no goal when running the race except to finish, but if I was being totally honest with myself, I wanted to get under four hours. Through the first eighteen miles I was on pace. Shortly after seeing my parents and kids I began to lose steam and had to keep reminding myself that I only had two more miles until I would see my school friends and gain a running mate.

Then, out of nowhere, as if an angel sent from above, Bekah, my cousin and running coach, appeared a full mile before she said she would. I cannot tell you what that did to my spirits. She was my smiling, lively burst of energy that I so desperately needed. We breezed through my friends at mile 20 and spent miles 21 and 22 chatting about Mill City Running, her new running store that she was hoping to open the next month.

I was favoring my knee, which was absolutely killing me at this point, but there was no way I was stopping now. They say that when you hit twenty miles in a marathon you are half done, and this is absolutely true. The first twenty felt ok (knee injury aside), and I felt like I was fully capable, but the last six, well, they were something straight out of a nightmare.

In my recollection of the last six miles, the wind had picked up, the sun was starting to scorch, and we were constantly running up-hill, though I am sure Bekah would describe a very different story. Thanks to Bekah distracting me from the agony and pain, before I knew it we were at mile 24, then 25, and finally 26.

At the 26-mile mark Bekah veered off to meet me at the finish line and I (now numb from the waist down) managed to speed up enough to look like a badass crossing the finish line . . . at 4:01:29. One minute late. Seriously?

As I sat on the grass, ice on my right knee and water in my hand, surrounded by my amazingly supportive family and friends, I was no longer a marathon virgin: I was a bona fide marathoner. I could count my name among the 0.5 percent of Americans that had accomplished this feat.

I had checked the biggest box off my bucket list and marked the occasion with a "twenty-six.two" tattoo across my left foot. This day was a big deal for me. It was all about me, about something I had spent months preparing for and had now accomplished.

I felt exceptional, which was pretty special for a girl who lives in the shadow of her crazy talented husband. But this day I was the one who was remarkable, and though I knew this feeling would only be temporary, it was my day, my accomplishment and something that no one could ever take away from me. That was enough for me, that one extra minute be damned.

I was not always a runner; far from it, to be honest. I was simply a sprinter in high school who never ran over 400 meters at once; I never considered whether I would have the capability to run a full marathon. Sure, the idea had always intrigued me, and it was number one on my bucket list, but it was nothing more than that—a hopeful "someday."

So what happened? How did this sprinter get to be a marathoner?

Well, after high school I had knee surgery my first year of college, and shortly after recovery, I decided I was going to run one to two miles a day to ward off the freshman 15. That was about the extent of my running experience. Then, not too long after I graduated college, I married a would-be professional baseball player for our hometown Minnesota Twins.

When Glen and I met he was a sweet, charming, albeit chubby, baseball player at the University of Minnesota. I was a headstrong, finally-single-for-the-first-time-in-my-serial-monogamist-life girl who was independent, with a subtle naiveté that made people think they needed to take care of me. He fell in love instantly; it took me a little longer, because I knew once I decided to date him I would marry him. Lo and behold we were engaged a mere two months after we started kissing. Going from best friends to forever was a simple move for us, and the best decision I have ever made. (Insert a collective "awww" here.)

Back to running, though. You need to understand that I have been surrounded by runners and running my whole life. My cousins, whom I grew up with and who are practically like sisters to me, are some of the most talented runners in the state of Minnesota. They tried countless times to get me to run in a family 4x400m relay in high school, but I always declined because 400m was way too far. (I highly regret this—we would have kicked butt. Sorry, cousins.)

My college roommate, Annie, was also a runner, which is how I ended up meeting Glen. I would do my best to get my two-mile runs in while Annie would bang out an hour of running like it was no big deal. I always longed to be like that but never understood it.

Then one day I did understand. To set the stage, it was 2011 and we were in the midst of our seventh spring in Fort Myers, Florida, with our two young daughters in tow. Spring training is a funny thing, because you are in a foreign city for two months with no friends except your teammates, and no babysitters. You get where I am going with this, right? It was me and the kids together, 24/7, for two months.

Since my kids were little and the days were too hot, we didn't go to the games. That year I never really saw many people other than my husband, which can do things to you. I was desperate for a conversation that didn't center around Dora, Goldfish crackers, or pacifiers. When Glen got home from the field he was hot and tired, but I was spent too and needed time away.

One day when he came home after work I headed out for a run, not knowing that this run would change my running trajectory forever.

I ran my usual two miles (the distance I had now determined was enough to allow me to eat chocolate and not gain weight), but I couldn't go home yet. I wasn't ready. I convinced myself to keep going. I ended up running five miles, a full two miles farther than I had ever run before.

Not only did I beat my personal best length that day in Florida, but something else happened on that run. For the first time ever I experienced "runner's high." I am sure you have heard of this elusive phenomenon—every runner talks about it. But until then I had had no idea what all the fuss was about. Every time someone mentioned it I played along, feeling as though I were faking an orgasm.

I had never experienced what everyone eluded to, but on this magical day, when I couldn't take one more minute with my kids (sorry, girls),

I had gotten there . . . found the big running O. Before those five miles I hated running. It felt too mundane and hard. But that was because I had never run long enough to get high.

That feeling makes you love running instead of loathe it. I tell everyone it happens after four miles, though that is just my theory. The high makes you want to keep going, makes you fall in love with each footstep, and leaves you intoxicated. Who'd have thought?

Something even greater happened for me out on that run, though: greater than the high was the release. The release of all this pent-up anxiety in my body that I hadn't found an outlet for until now.

My doctor told me when I was first diagnosed with anxiety that I had high levels of adrenaline running through my body; had I not had really low blood pressure they likely would have put me on a beta-blocker instead of an antianxiety med. In running I had found a way to release that pent-up adrenaline that did not involve bringing my heart to a near stop.

I entered the house that day feeling at ease and calm, something I hadn't felt in a very long time. I was hooked. Right then and there I knew I was on to something. Glen could tell, too. He saw a more relaxed, calm, easy wife—and he liked it.

To this day, when we argue, he will casually say, "Hey, when was the last time you went for a run?" He knows I can run it out and then whatever we were arguing about won't seem like such a big deal. He calls me his own springer spaniel; sometimes I just need to run.

So now I was going to be a "runner."

> "How do you run away from things
> that are in your head?"
> –Unknown

...

GOLDY'S 10-MILE RACE

April 9, 2011

Let's go back to the beginning, because even with the date above I am getting ahead of myself. I just gave you a quick synopsis of how I became a runner, and after that first "long" run in spring training, I was full steam ahead. I was a "runner" now, after all. Truth be told, the word still frightens me. I feel like there is a stigma attached to it, like I have to prove something. I felt the fear and did it anyway. (My therapist would be proud.)

I decided to sign up for my first official 10-mile race that April in hopes of doing my first half marathon shortly thereafter. Running a full marathon had been one of the very few items on my bucket list since I was a kid, and for the first time in my life I believed it was a true possibility. I was hooked, and there was no stopping me.

I am a fighter, and I always accomplish whatever I set my mind to. This was going to be no different—26.2, here I come—but first, of course, I had to get through less than half of it: 10 miles.

I started training, while slowly inching toward the 7-mile mark. I was encouraged by the way I was feeling mentally, but it was not as easy physically. It was a struggle to add that half mile each week in spring training, pushing my body just a bit further than it had ever gone. There were definitely times when I felt like I couldn't do it, but tenacity prevailed and I would somehow make it.

Shortly before leaving Florida I had managed to hit the 7-mile mark. It was not always pretty, but I got it done. There was a lot of chafing from my inner-thigh chub rub, and my feet were starting to look like the feet of those biblical men who didn't wear shoes. I am sure my husband was longing for the days when my toenail polish actually stayed on and covered up the mess that was happening on my toes.

Chafing and blisters showed my progress, but I was still scared to death as I headed up to the University of Minnesota for my very first 10-mile race.

It was the inaugural year of Goldy's 10 Mile, and as I toed the starting line I felt the sudden urge to throw up. (Apparently this is a theme of mine during new race distances.) I had trained for this, but I had only run up to seven miles. Bekah had promised me the adrenaline would get me through those last three.

I had no goals going into this race except to finish. I was going to start off really slow for fear I would die at the end if I didn't. I remember milling around before we began; there was an older man next to me in his sixties, and he must have seen the stress written all over my face, because he struck up a conversation with me. I informed him that this was my first race and that I was kind of freaking out. He told me this was his first race back since having knee-replacement surgery, and suggested that maybe we could run together to start. This idea mellowed me enough to be able to keep the vomit down.

We lasted probably two miles together, me and my new friend, and as I finally peeled away from him I turned back and smiled. He gave me a thumbs-up as we parted. I never saw him again, though I did look for him at the finish. He had a profound effect on me that day. The comfort his presence brought me is not something I will easily forget. He was there for me at a time when I needed someone, and I never even knew his name. Runners are like that, though, a tight-knit group. We bond over the waves we give each other as we run by and the commiserating smiles we exchange out on the road. There is no need for words; we know what the other is feeling, and give a nod, wave, or smile as a sign of our mutual respect for the miles we are all putting in.

As I ran through my old stomping grounds and saw all the changes that had occurred in the six years since I had graduated, it dawned on me how much I had changed as well.

Up until this point, our life had been focused on Glen's career, which in turn affected our family. Honestly, baseball was our life. As much as I did not want it to take over, it had. How could it not? I fought long and hard against it. I wanted so badly to be something other than just a baseball wife. So I started a videography company before I had kids, a tutu company and temporary-tattoo company when the kids were young, and would eventually head up a race.

Anxiety usually rears its head in the quiet times, which is why people with anxiety enjoy being busy. They search out things to do or be a part of so they don't have time to be alone and think. That was the case for me, anyway; I was so busy trying to ward off my thoughts that I was willing to undertake anything. It is still a constant struggle for me, and I have a repetitive cycle that I tend to go through. I overbook to prevent downtime, time that could lead to too much thinking, and then I get worn down from the amount of things I have going on and so I shut down. I close ranks and spend the day on the couch watching TV and napping while the kids are at school. No calls, no texts, no writing, no emails, no friends, no thinking . . . just mindless TV until I can get back on my feet.

It is an awful cycle and one I am ashamed of. I hate the days I spend doing nothing; the type A in me can't handle it. Glen, on the other hand, loves these days for me, thinks I desperately need them, and applauds me when I take them. There is a middle ground, one that I am trying all the time to find, where I don't shut down but I do allow myself to slow down without fear of where my mind will go. I need to realize that I can do anything but not everything.

In the end, for us to be a cohesive family unit, I had to give up everything to be Glen's wife and the mother of our children. I thrived in the role, but until I found running I hadn't found my voice. I felt competent but not complete.

It had been all about Glen and the kids for such a long time that I hadn't even remembered to think about me. Here I was now, doing something just for me at the place where it all began for us. I knew that after this race things would be different. I wouldn't forget about me. As a mom, I would probably never put myself first, but I would make sure my needs were in the mix.

Taking care of one's self is so incredibly important, but it is one of the hardest things to do; taking care of others is much easier. Really taking the time to figure out who you are and what exactly you need takes some intense focus inward, which can reveal things about yourself you may not always like. But it is necessary. We moms need to remember that taking care of ourselves is part of taking care of our kids. Like the flight attendant always says, "Place your oxygen mask on before assisting others." Even they know that breathing is important, and without it, life stops.

Every time I run I try to focus on my breath and think about that very fact, that it is what is keeping me alive. It is you, your breath, and the open road. Running gave me a purpose, gave me back a piece of me, and a voice all my own, and for that I am forever grateful.

I finished the race in 1:37:21. I was exhausted, excited, dripping with sweat, yet chilled from the air. My feet hurt and my body was spent. I like to think I was looking pretty good at that point, but I think it was the runner's high creating an illusion, because the pictures show a different story.

After that race I was hooked. I went home and signed up for my very first half marathon just two months away. The feeling I got crossing that finish line was overwhelming. There is something about the "finish-line feeling" that just can't be described. It is a moment where exhaustion meets euphoria meets knowing you can finally use the bathroom. It is the moment when all your adrenaline is depleted and all that is left is jubilation. It was the calmest and least anxious I had felt in years.

I have battled with anxiety since the birth of our first child. Being pregnant changes so much about your body, which I already resent-ed, but it hadn't occurred to me that it could change your mind as well. I was not one of those women who enjoyed being pregnant; it wasn't that my pregnancy was hard or awful, but it was uncom-fortable and I wanted my body back as mine. This once skinny, cute, bubbly girl was fat, had acne not just on my face but in places you didn't even know you could get acne, and an attitude that I am sure made Glen wonder who this monster was that he had married.

Basically, to me, pregnancy was a means to an end—an amazing end—but an end nonetheless. The fact that it left me with scars, extra fat, mood swings, and a mental shift was not thrilling, but it is what it is.

I remember the moment clear as day. The moment where anxiety gripped me hard.

It was 2007, our daughter Addie was almost one, and one of my neighbors was over visiting with me while the kids played. She ca-sually mentioned, "Hey, did you hear about the thing with the police the next block over the other night?"

I had no idea what she was talking about, and so she continued.

"Apparently, a few days ago, a woman was raped by her neighbor's son in the morning after her husband went to work. Her husband had left the front door unlocked, and so the neighbor walked right in, up to the bedroom, put his hand over her mouth, a knife to her throat, and proceeded to rape her while her young daughter slept down the hall. Awful, isn't it?"

I could not believe it. A rape? In Lakeville? Seriously?

Lakeville was where I grew up, where my parents met, even where my grandparents met. To me it was as "Andy Griffith" as you can get. It was a big city with a small-town feel, and was a safe place to raise kids. This was the place where I used to ride my bike downtown to my cashier job at Erickson Drug, the local drugstore. Think of a five-and-dime; that was where I spent my preteens raking in the dough. Things like this didn't happen in Lakeville; they just didn't.

She went on to tell me that the police had arrested the suspect and that there was no threat to the neighborhood because it wasn't a random assault. The victim had been his only target. He had been watching her for months.

I was reeling. What was this feeling? Why couldn't I let this go?

Logically, there was nothing to worry about. He was in jail, and he only wanted her. He didn't want to assault me. So why was I spinning out of control?

The ironic part was that I had spent four years in college at the U of M in Minneapolis, a place far less safe than Lakeville, and I had rarely given two thoughts to the bad things going on around me.

This is not to say I didn't exercise caution. My doors were always locked, and I rarely walked home alone at night. (Sorry, Mom, but it did happen from time to time.) But even though acts of violence had occurred on campus, the threat to my safety had never bothered me.

So why did this?

I became obsessed with the story. I would drive by the house that she lived in, read all the newspaper stories I could find about the assault, and pried more information out of my neighbors. Of course my neighbors had long since moved on and blown it off, but the threat was still very real to me.

When I couldn't find more information I would watch the news and read the newspaper to find out about other bad things happening around the state nowhere near me. I needed to know anyway. I had this irrational thought that if I read about assaults I would be prepared when it happened to me—and at this point I was convinced that it would.

Why couldn't I be the "one" that this happened to? I was sure I was next.

The anxiety latched on and latched on hard—so hard that I had to have my mom sleep at my house with me every time Glen was on the road (which was a lot). I needed her not just at my house but actually in the same bed. I was living in constant fear, a gripping fear that wouldn't allow me to leave the house without overthinking the heck out of it.

What if they bomb the Mall of America while I am there? What if a shooter comes into the movie theater? Something was going to happen. It was just a matter of time.

Glen, being type B and easygoing, did not understand what I was feeling and why I was suddenly insane. He did a great job of trying to be logical with me, and reminded me that I lived in a safe community and I was going to be all right.

The funny part is I understood all of that. Logically, I knew this was all a little nuts and a waste of time, but the anxiety part of me did not stop. Later my therapist would describe this as the double-noose effect. It was like having two nooses around your neck, the logical one and the anxious one.

The logical one is pulling one way and telling you, "This is nuts, you are fine, nothing is going to happen to you," but the anxious one says, "Why can't you be the one? This could happen. Why not you?"

You get stuck in the middle, and you cannot remove either noose. So you tailspin, getting nowhere and going nowhere—except deeper into this hell of your own creation.

This was when I began seeing a therapist, a wonderful woman whom I sometimes refer to as my best friend. I still see her to this day, seven years later. The things she has talked me through and taught me are incredible. I am a sucker for "bettering myself," whether that is by exercising, changing eating habits, or working on my mind, so therapy was right up my alley.

I was struggling with what was going on with me. It seemed to come out of left field, and I was so frustrated that I could not control it. See, that is the funny thing about anxiety—it is a perpetual cycle. It starts, you want to control it, you can't control it, you get stressed that you can't control it, and so it gets worse . . . it spirals and spirals.

This anxiety manifested into an obsession with the idea that someone was going to do something to my kids. Because my husband was a public figure, I felt we were a target and, therefore, that it was more likely that something bad would happen to us. I would lie in bed at night and conjure up the most intense scenarios based on the slightest noise that I would hear, all the while figuring out how I would get to Addie in her room across the hall when this all went down.

I changed all the main numbers in my cell phone to references Addie would know in case something happened to me and she needed to call "Nana" instead of "Mom," as my mom was previously listed in my phone, or "Dad" instead of "Glen."

Truth be told, the contacts in my phone are still written that way, and it provides a sense of security even though I know it shouldn't.

When I entered the elementary education program at the University of Minnesota, I needed to find a volunteer job. Looking through the campus brochure, The Jacob Wetterling Foundation caught my eye immediately.

For those of you who don't know, Jacob Wetterling was an eleven-year-old boy who was abducted one night in Minnesota while riding his bike with friends. To this day they have never found him, or have any idea what could have happened to him. A cold case in child abduction.

The case rocked the state of Minnesota, and I remember wearing a shirt featuring his elementary school picture that read, "We are Jacob's hope"; I was only a few grades below him. There is not a single person who lived in Minnesota in the 1990s who does not know of the Jacob Wetterling case. This was every mom's worst nightmare, and my mom was no different.

Here was a foundation with an intention to set right the tragedies that had occurred in my youth and were still happening today. If

Patty Wetterling couldn't bring Jacob back, she was going to make sure this did not happen to other children.

The stories I heard during my time there did nothing to calm the anxiety that was flooding in, all because of some stupid story about a neighbor I had never even met. It wasn't until later in life that I would really see the impact of my time there on my psyche. Unbeknownst to me, this was the beginning of my long battle with anxiety.

Without my knowledge, my mother also had anxiety, something she hid really well, which is characteristic of that generation. I think the Jacob Wetterling story really set my mom off, got her head spinning over fears that no mother should have to worry about, and made her forever overly worried about her kids. Imagine how that abduction would have affected me. I would have lost it.

I vividly remember watching several "Don't talk to strangers" videos in elementary school (and can still sing all the words to the *Winnie the Pooh* version—maybe it should be my go-to karaoke tune). My mom drove the fear of God into us that if we did not stay by her side when we were out, someone would take us and we would never see her or my dad again. This can be a helpful strategy when you are sick and tired of your kids running off while you are trying to grocery shop, but since I was a young kid with underlying anxiety issues, it caused a real problem for me.

I followed what she said when I was young, scared to death someone was going to take me. As I got older and the "invincible" teen and college years set in, I was more reckless and more willing to throw caution to the wind. In college my mom would try to call me, and if I was at class or napping and did not call her back immediately (this was before you could text), she would call my roommate and any other friends whose numbers she had, to make sure I was not dead. After all, I was going to school in Minneapolis, and to her that was worlds away from Lakeville.

Listen, I am not blaming my mom for my fear of bad people; in fact, I am thankful that she told us the truth while we were young. I have known others who grew up naïve to the ways of the world, and though my thoughts may be more skeptical when it comes to people's intentions, at least I know to take precautions so I won't be attacked.

But more on that later. Back to running.

"Of course it is happening inside your head . . .
but why on earth should that mean that it is not real?"
−Albus Dumbledore

...

MINNEAPOLIS HALF MARATHON

June 5, 2011

My very first half marathon, the Minneapolis Half, an accomplishment I had wondered if I would ever achieve. I was dressed to kill in my first pair of running capris from Lululemon and the matching tank top to boot; you might even say I was looking cute. I was certain that this new gear was going to help streamline my performance. Hadn't that been what the salesperson had said, after all? That these expensive crops and shirt were going to shave minutes off my time?

Since running Goldy's 10 Mile I had gotten hooked. I went home that night, found the first half marathon in the Twin Cities that I could attend, and signed up. As I write this, a little wiser in the ways of racing, I know how important it is to really research the race that you are going to run. You need to look at so many factors before you sign on the dotted line and pay the fees, because most races are nonrefundable. Needless to say, when it came to this race, I did not do my due diligence.

First, look at the date. Does it work with your schedule? What will the weather be like that time of year? What time does the race start?

Next, look at the terrain. Most races have their course map and elevation map on their website. It is good to have an idea of what you have in store: Will the course be flat? Hilly? Through the city or the country? Although, I admit, sometimes it is better if you don't know; knowing that the worst is still to come can sometimes backfire.

Then look at the previous year's results to see what the finish times were and how many people ran it. You can decide based on the race size if it is what you are looking for.

Last, check out the swag and other gimmicks of the run. Does it come with a fun medal or cool shirt? Are there lots of spectators? Double-check that you are ok with the price, because odds are, you are not getting that money back even if you can't run it. I have signed up for my fair share of races that I didn't end up running, so make sure you are in it for the long haul, because races are not cheap. They say you are a real runner when you scoff at spending $40 to go to the movies and get snacks but have no problem coughing up $50 for a 5k that lasts only twenty-five minutes.

The high I experienced during Goldy's 10 Mile was like nothing I had ever felt. The release of the pent-up anxiety, adrenaline, and stress was better than an orgasm. (Don't tell Glen.) I had been looking for a long time for something like this. I had tried just about everything to ease my anxiety. I had been seeing my therapist for about two years at the time and loved every minute of it. I felt I had a decent handle on things and my progress was good, but I still was struggling. The anxiety had gotten progressively worse with each of my two kids until I finally reached a breaking point in 2009.

It was another one of those "clear as day" memories (and for a girl with a terrible memory, this is impressive). It was the very first week of January and we were headed to my parents' house from our house, a mere three-mile drive. It was snowing lightly and there was just enough snow to cover the road. Glen was driving and the girls were buckled up and snuggled in their car seats in the back watching VeggieTales.

I remember sitting in the passenger seat, filled with so much worry that Glen was going to slide us off the road in the snow. I started to feel my chest tighten and my breathing speed up. I hated not being in control, even as I realized Glen would obviously drive safe and would never want anything to happen to us. Still, I felt like I should be driving, that I should be in control.

By the time we got to my parents' I was on the edge of a full-out panic attack. It was right then and there that I realized therapy was not going to be enough for me. I had been seeing my amazing therapist for two years pretty much weekly, and though I loved her and had gotten a lot out of our sessions, it was clear in this moment that I needed medication in order to deal with this.

I went to the doctor right away. I am one of those people who goes to the doctor to prevent things instead of treat them. I have never understood how people can just wait until crap hits the fan to go to the doctor. I want to see it coming, preferably from a long way away.

This is not possible—to know the future, that is—but nonetheless I still get my annual Pap smear to know for at least a year that I am hopefully ok. So I went to my OB and told her everything. That is the other thing about me—I am pretty honest, an open book. I am who I am and I make no apologies. (Well, that's not totally true; I am a people pleaser to a fault.)

I don't believe in regrets and think everything that happens and everything that you choose to do shapes who you are. So I had no problem telling my OB. She did not seem too surprised given the family history and the increasing symptoms with each pregnancy.

I was prescribed 10mg of Lexapro, at which point she told me that, unfortunately, there is no neurotransmitter testing. Doctors have to guess which chemical is low in your brain and blindly prescribe a drug to help. I was supposed to give the medicine three months and report back. The thing that struck me the most about this conversation was the fact that the medical world can perform heart transplants but they still have not developed a way to test the neurotransmitter levels in your brain. How is this possible? The only good thing to come from all these recent shootings is that mental health has been pushed to the forefront, and with this hopefully to will the ability to test for it.

I asked how I would know it was working, to which she replied that this was not one of those situations where I would magically feel better the next day. Instead, I would look back after a few weeks and realize things hadn't been so stressful, not so many "what ifs," and I would feel more "normal." Whatever "normal" feels like, I guess. If that was not the case after three months, we would try another drug.

For those of you shaking your head at the idea of taking drugs, I get it, I do. I need you to understand I am a big opponent of taking drugs. I barely take Motrin for a headache, and the idea of taking meds every day did not sit well with me at all. But my doctor said, "Alisha, I have high cholesterol, runs in my family. I eat well, run, and I cannot get my numbers to go down, so I have to take a pill for it. Your anxiety is no different. It is beyond something that you can control; it is a deficiency in your body. If you have to take a pill to live a better life, take the damn pill."

So I took the damn pill.

The doctor was right—I was not magically cured. Instead I began to notice that each day I was not so on edge. I felt like the Lexapro brought me down to a "normal" level, and I was able to process everyday conflicts in a more natural manner instead of trying to get through the day at a level 10.

I slept better and was a better mother, wife, and friend. Overall I was much easier to deal with, and I recognized it—as did those around me. I had no problem telling my family and friends about my anxiety. I did not think it was something to hide, and I was not ashamed about something I could not control.

One of my friends even bought me a hand towel with a 1950s housewife on it holding a pie. Next to her are the words "medicated and motivated." I loved it because that was me; I was kicking butt and feeling good. Though I still was not super into the idea of taking this damn pill every day, I kept on keeping on.

I felt I had found the magic concoction: therapy, the damn pill, and running. I would never have believed that part of the solution to my mental illness would lie in physical exercise, but here I was longing to run farther and cross that half-marathon line. My therapist later told me it didn't surprise her at all that running was helping; she sees its benefits in a lot of her patients. The release counteracts the anxiety and can leave people feeling more Zen. I was Zen all right, at least when I ran, and I wanted to be even more so. I craved it.

To be real, I don't remember much about the Minneapolis Half Marathon except a massive hill that just about took me down. (Remember Sign-up Protocol 101?) I like to think that I was so consumed with sheer joy that it all blurred together, but really I was just trying to get through it. The race was hard, much harder than I expected. Anyone who tells you it is easy is lying. I have been doing this long enough to tell you that running is not always easy or fun. The moments that it is are the ones that keep you hooked. Running is relatively simple but it is not easy, and that's the beauty in it.

What I do know is that I did get through it, crossed the finish line in 2:02:42, and promptly went home and signed up for the next half marathon. I was half-crazy and fully committed.

"The greatest act of courage is to be and own all that you are. Without apology, without excuses, without masks to cover the truth of who you really are."

-Unknown

...

MINNESOTA HALF MARATHON

August 6, 2011

It had been two months since I toed my very first half-marathon starting line, and I had decided that this race I was going to run faster. I was no longer a half-marathon virgin, but a real-deal running machine. I would hit the pavement whenever I could, both kids in the huge double jogging stroller, and just run, with all 75–100 pounds that I was pushing in front of me. It became routine in our house. I would grab blankets, iPods, and snacks, and the kids would play on their screens or sleep while Mom ran. Usually we ran to a park that was two and a half miles away, where the kids would get out and play (and I would get a welcome break). Then we ran the two and a half miles back.

All those five-mile treks with the stroller brought me mental peace but physical exhaustion. When I look back on this, several years since pushing that darn stroller in front of me, I cannot believe I ever did this; the thought of it seems so hard now tells you how much I must of needed it mentally. I was so used to not using my arms to run for so many years that when I finally got rid of the stroller I pictured myself looking like Brad Pitt in *Burn After Reading*, when he is dancing while running on the treadmill. I was certain that this weird swinging sensation made me look like a fool.

There is such a mind-body connection that comes with running. You start to see your body in a different way. The more you run, the more you love your body. Not that I ever feel it is perfect—in fact, far from it—but because with every mile my body proves to me that I am more capable than I ever thought possible. You start to get a whole new respect for your body. It is not about losing weight or how you look after a run; it is about how running makes you feel. You push your body to the limits, and when your legs quit, you run with your heart. The connection is there—you just need to find it.

The Minnesota Half Marathon was to be only the second half I ever attempted. I had again made the mistake of not doing my due diligence when it came to checking all the background information on this race, and I was in for quite a treat on the back half, with a hill that lives in infamy in my mind. I remember running along, not really enjoying myself, and then it appeared . . . this massive uphill in front of me. People ahead were all walking, and I was nervous just looking at it. Let me tell you, it is so hard not to walk when everyone around you has given in; talk about mental toughness. I began my ascent, and while it took everything I had—I think I only walked for one stretch—I did finally make it to the top. Wouldn't you know, there sat my parents, waiting to cheer me on. My mom said, "Pretty steep hill, huh?" and I couldn't even respond. I was spent (thanks captain obvious).

This wouldn't be the end of my uphill battle on this race. The last half mile was a gradual uphill. To any race director who may be reading this right now, that is not a good idea—in fact, it is a horrid one. Just when you think you are almost done and you start to get your last kick, you are hit with a nasty hill. Really? Whoever signed off on that course must have been fired, because by the next year they had changed the course and the race no longer ended on a hill. I guess I will just look back at it now as "character building." Isn't that how we should look at anything that doesn't go our way?

Glen is gone a lot, baseball life is crazy, and sometimes it feels like the only thing I can count on is inconsistency and running. At this point in early August we were in the heart of the baseball season, the part where it really starts to take its toll on me. I miss my husband, miss his help, and start to feel the void. Running truly has filled a void in my life that I didn't know how to deal with. It has helped me deal with the baseball life and all the difficulties that that life poses for a family. I used to always feel like something was off; I never really fit into the typical "professional athlete's wife" mold. I always wanted to be more. Sure, I was a wife and a mother to two amazing girls, and for a long time this sufficed. I was content but not complete. I was not sure what was missing. Turns out I was missing my voice, and somehow or another running has given it back to me.

Our life in baseball has not always been easy; Glen and I have experienced the highest highs and the lowest lows. There have been times when we were on the outside looking in, and were public enemy number one. We grew up, clawed our way back in, fought hard, kept our heads down, and tried to maintain a little dignity in the process. Along the way we clung tightly to each other, focused on our family, and tried to fit into this crazy baseball world we felt we weren't equipped for.

From the beginning I could tell I was not going to be a stereotypical baseball wife. I never seemed to fit in, to be like them. Baseball was a job to me and Glen, and we strived to keep it that way. We didn't want it to creep into our "real life." We kept our kids on a "normal life" schedule, which is the opposite of the baseball schedule. The baseball schedule consists of bringing your kids to the game and putting them in the player day care until Dad's game is done. Then you wait for Dad to get his act together and get out of the locker room, which means by the time you get home it is close to midnight and the whole family goes to bed and then sleeps in together until 10 a.m. or so. This schedule is awesome for the dads, because they get to see their kids after the games, but it just did not sit right with us to keep our kids up that late, and once they began school, this was just not possible.

Since Glen is now the closer and does not come in until the very end of the game (which is usually close to 10 p.m.), by the time I would have sat through the game, watched him, and got home, I wouldn't have been to bed until midnight—only to get up at 7 a.m. to get our kids ready for school. Anyone who knows me knows that if there is one thing I take seriously it is sleep. Recently, for Mother's Day, when asked "If I had a million dollars, what would I buy my mom?" my daughter Addie answered with "A twenty-four-hour nap." See? Even my kids know that me + sleep = bliss. I still like to think we are putting our kids to bed at 7 p.m. for them and not for me. I'd be lying if I said I didn't love it, though. Momma needs her downtime . . . wine and *Scandal* are calling my name.

The weeks of running with the stroller and enforcing early bedtimes had brought me to my second half marathon in 2011, the Minnesota Half. I knew this time what to expect, and that took the guesswork out of it, which eased my mind. Since the first race I had become a running fiend, running sometimes seven days a week. I had come a long way since I first put a name to my disorder and my feet to the pavement, and I knew I was on to something. This was a new beginning for me.

Other than the hills, nothing too exciting happened, but I did get it done a little faster . . . 1:56:45.

> "I bend so I don't break."
> —Unknown

...

13.1 MINNEAPOLIS

August 21, 2011

Only two weeks after I ran the Minnesota Half I was at it again. I was desperate to keep my running streak going, so I signed up for the 13.1 Minneapolis. This would be the last year of this race, and so I was on the cusp of history. I had heard good things about the 13.1 race series and was excited to see if I could go a little faster and maybe even learn to take time to look around while I ran. This course ran me from my favorite starting point in Minneapolis (St. Anthony Main) down along the river roads and through some of the prettiest parts of the city.

I remember loving the course and trying to breathe it in. This race was smaller than those I had run before, only about 1,600 participants, which thrilled and scared me. I was scared because I did not want to come in last and look like an idiot, and thrilled because there were not as many people to make your way around during the race. I am a middle-of-the-pack runner, not in the front, and usually not in the back, but I was still nervous about this. I was not sure how I would feel after. I will tell you, that race taught me that I like the smaller races.

During this race something incredible happened. I know what you are thinking: "Seriously? You already described the big running orgasm. What could be better than that?" I hear ya, but stay with me.

While running for hours (literally), you have a lot of time to think. While I usually try to focus on the music or do math to see what my finish time will be (dorky, I know, but it works), this time I got lost in another thought completely. I was stewing, my mind was given some time to run, and as the worries fell on the pavement it made way for my creative mind to be free.

Running had done so much for me—given me a voice, kept my anxiety in check, and given me a sense of peace I didn't know existed. In that moment, during that race, I wanted to give back to running; I wanted to spread the love. I wanted others to feel what I felt, know what I now knew about this amazing release. I wanted to inspire people to get out there, get active, and maybe tie it all together with a great cause. Glen and I have always wanted to use baseball for a greater purpose, use our unique platform for good. Here in 2011, things were finally on the upswing for Glen after a lot of time down in the trenches, and we wanted to give back to those who helped get us there. We were grateful for what we had and wanted to share the wealth.

A few players had their own events they held for charity, and of course there were the many wives events throughout the year in which we helped give back. The thing about these events was that usually you had to pay a pretty penny to get in the door, and we wanted to do something for everyone—especially families.

I had recently run the Minnesota Twins Territory 4k in August of 2011, and was not overly impressed with the event; I felt it left a lot to be desired. I wanted to make it longer, more fun, include the current players, and get people running who otherwise would not be. During this very race, my 13.1, I cooked up a plan to revamp the current race and make it our own—this time with a charitable cause and a family-friendly vibe. I eventually sold the idea to the Twins front office, and by February of 2012 we had nailed down a name, date, and recipient for the very first race Glen and I would organize.

Fifteen's 5k would take place on August 12, 2012, and all proceeds would benefit the Cystic Fibrosis Foundation. CFF was close to our hearts because Glen and I have two sets of friends who have little ones with CF, and it breaks our hearts to see the lengths these parents have to go to for their kids just to live a seminormal life. We have gone out to lunch with them, and I have watched Jess have to sanitize the heck out of the tray and not allow Landry to carry it in an effort to prevent germ exposure. Then you look over at my kids and they are darn near licking the trays without giving one thought to it. We wanted to help them get closer to a cure. This race was going to become a reality, all because of the free time along the miles of the 13.1 Minneapolis.

I even managed to shave two minutes off my time . . . 1:54:01.

I did not have another race on the docket until the end of October, so I needed a way to stay motivated and in top shape. I was still running a lot at this point, anywhere from four to seven days a week, but the monotony of the miles was taking its toll and I needed something to break up the repetitiveness.

Lo and behold a friend and I got to chatting, and she mentioned this new class she was doing called Yoga Sculpt. She wanted me to come try it and promised it would kick my ass. I was hesitant because I had done yoga before, and the "ohm meditation" stretching was just not for me. Not to mention that while I was supposed to be letting my mind quiet down, instead I was sitting there thinking about all the things I should have been doing instead of taking this darn class.

I am not a stretcher. As far back as high school I very rarely stretched before I ran. I know some of you are cringing at this, and I get it, but I have never really felt the need so I just don't do it. I remember in high school walking over to the chain-link fence that surrounded the track and swinging my leg, like, five times to make it look like I was doing what everyone else was, but I was rolling my eyes the whole time.

In my defense, there is a lot of research disputing stretching (especially static) and its benefits versus its disadvantages. Everyone has their opinions and everyone knows what works for their body. Maybe as I get older I will feel differently about it, but for now I am on the "just head out the door and run" camp, no stretching required.

With this mentality and my previous "way too Zen for this type A gal" yoga experience, my friend had an uphill battle to try and get me to this new-age yoga class with her. But after much poking (remember when you could do that on Facebook?) and prodding, she finally twisted my arm.

Arriving to Yoga Sculpt for the first time, I could tell immediately that this was not your mother's yoga class. The class was so packed with people that there were only about two inches separating each person's mat, and the music was pumping so loud that you didn't immediately notice the room was a humid 95 degrees.

Notice it you did, though. It kind of smacked you in the face, and you started sweating just sitting there. Not too long after we unrolled our mats and grabbed some five-pound weights, our instructor came in and we began. He was a cute, young, in-shape guy who spent the next sixty minutes thoroughly kicking our ass while sweat dripped down to the floor almost to the beat of the music that was pounding the walls.

By the end, after our ears were still ringing from "Pour Some Sugar on Me," we had done 120 pushups, enough planks to make it hard to even laugh the next day, and so much cardio that it felt as though we had run five miles. I don't think I walked normally for a week after, but you can bet that I was back in his class the next week for another ass-kicking. I loved the intensity of it and convinced my mom and some other friends to do it with me. Before long we were all hooked.

I like to think that these workouts benefited my running because, as you will see, I started to get faster. I was getting stronger and it was helping me speed up. Or maybe it was the sneaky stretching—but I will never admit to that.

> "You have brains in your head, you have feet in your shoes,
> you can steer yourself in any direction you choose."
> –Dr. Seuss

...

MONSTER DASH HALF MARATHON

October 29, 2011

I was ready to run my last half marathon of 2011 after having banged out three already. The Monster Dash Half Marathon was not a hard sell at all; in fact, I think I signed up on the day registration opened. Not only was the course extremely intriguing, winding you through Summit Avenue, where you can ogle the huge mansions, the cathedral, and the capitol—not to mention it is all slightly downhill—but throw in people dressed up in creative costumes and I was all in.

I knew I could not run this race sans costume, so as soon as I signed up I got to work picking one out. I will admit it is hard to pick out a costume that is appropriate to run in, never mind the fact that it was going to be a chilly 20-degree morning on race day. I needed something that wouldn't chafe, wouldn't be too cold, wouldn't be too hot, and wouldn't drive me crazy for the next thirteen miles . . . no small feat, for sure. I eventually landed on an Oscar the Grouch costume. No rhyme or reason for it besides the fact that it met the criteria and seemed semi-cute. So on the chilly morning of October 29 I donned a fuzzy green outfit with some equally fuzzy leg warmers

39

and headed to the state capitol in St. Paul for what I was sure would be a fun race.

I was right. That race was pure fun from start to finish, minus the trash-can headpiece that bounced up and down with every stride. The costumes were incredible; I saw a trio of guys dressed as huge Q-tips, too many superheroes to count, cartoon characters, scientists, Thing 1 & 2, characters from *Dumb and Dumber*, and just about every Disney princess ever.

The course was spectacular. It started near the cathedral in St. Paul, snaked through some of the prettiest neighborhoods that St. Paul has to offer, and glided us along the banks of the river. A beautifully crisp autumn day in October . . . perfect race weather.

The best part of all was that this was the first race that my husband and kiddos attended. Glen is pretty much not around from February to the end of September. We have a piece of art in our house that says, "We interrupt this family to bring you the baseball season," and it couldn't be truer. He misses out on a lot, which is hard, but knowing he will be retired before we are forty and that we will be financially stable is a great trade-off.

Since my running streak had started he had not been able to see me in action, so this was fun for both of us. I have spent my life cheering him on; now the roles were reversed. Being Glen's wife meant taking a backseat and holding down the fort while he did his thing, and while I was ok with this for a long time, I knew in my heart I wanted more. I wanted to accomplish something all mine. To be able to accomplish something in front of my girls felt pretty awesome, too. For my girls to see that sense of achievement on my face made me

prouder than any race time could have. I wanted them to lo
me; I wanted to be a great role model. This was one of those times
when you feel like maybe you are doing one thing right as a parent.

It didn't hurt that I ran my fastest time yet, a quick 1:44:12; 7:56
a mile. I was pretty blown away with my drop in time, a whole ten
minutes faster than my last race. Since the 13.1 Minneapolis I had
teamed up with Bekah to create a plan to make me faster. I had
reservations as to whether I could get any faster, but I followed the
plan anyway, and it worked. Before hiring her as my coach I would
just run to run. I would run the same pace every day whether I was
running four miles or eleven. This, I learned, is a recipe for injury and
a plateau. I was not really getting any better, and I was starting to feel
aches and pains but did not know why.

I have since read several running books and learned the importance
of speed, tempo, and strength runs. Running the same pace every
day is fine, but if you want to get faster, fitter, thinner, better, you
need to change it up and push your body. If the fact that I cut almost
a minute a mile off my times in only two months doesn't convince
you to try it, I don't know what will. If you want more information
on this type of training but don't have the money to hire a coach,
you should buy *Hansons Marathon Method* by Luke Humphrey. He
goes much more in depth on this topic and even gives you specific
workouts you can do. Seriously, buy it now.

This race was also where I fell in love with listening to books on tape
while out on the open road. Honestly, I had listened to many books
on tape while "out on the open road" during the times I drove Glen's
car across the country while moving from minor-league team to
minor-league team. I feel like I spent most of 2005 to 2007 driving

the highways of the United States. Glen had moved up the minor-league ladder fast, and when he had to go to the next team I was left to clean up, pack up, and drive everything to our next "home" until we had to do it again.

The minor leagues in baseball are a humbling time. You are living much like college kids but with the craziest instability you have ever seen. I am talking three to four guys in a two-bedroom apartment, spitters all over, eating boxes of cereal and ramen to pinch pennies. Glen was lucky enough to get a good signing bonus, so we could eat more than dehydrated noodles, but it was still simple living at its best. You can go from one team to the next in as short as a day. As someone with undiagnosed anxiety, this time in our life was a struggle for me. As life goes, though, I did not have a choice, so I sucked it up, got in the car, and drove. Those long hours on the road left too much time for my mind to wander, and so at one stop somewhere in Tennessee I bought my first book on tape, *Confessions of a Shopaholic* by Sophie Kinsella.

Those next six hours flew by, and before I knew it I was on the side of the road searching on my Sidekick (remember those?) for another bookstore to get more books on tape. I was hooked. The books kept my wandering mind at bay and helped me navigate those long treks across the country.

I don't know why it didn't click earlier for me that the same philosophy would apply to running, but once it did, I was all in. I rarely listen to music when I run now; I am usually knee-deep in a book. Listening to books on tape also bodes well for conversations, because you come off as all kinds of worldly once you have "read" all these books. But that's a secret we can keep between us.

"Broken crayons still color."
–Unknown

...

LULULEMON HOT TODDIES RUN

December 4, 2011

I have to admit that once I was a half-marathon runner it never dawned on me that I could run races that were shorter than that. That is how I am sometimes. I get so wrapped up in looking beyond the horizon that I miss the obvious. I would never describe myself as flighty (although my hubby may call me out on that), but I think sometimes I am too many steps ahead to realize what is at hand. At this point I was only focused on the one milestone further: the elusive full marathon. However, in late November of 2011, while shopping at Lululemon (third in my list of addictions, behind only Amazon and Starbucks), one of the employees told me that I should come run their "Hot Toddies" run.

This run was to take place in the dead of winter in St. Paul. The premise was to wear the shortest shorts possible and run down Grand Avenue with the promise of a hot toddy drink to warm our buns at the end. I am never one to shy away from a challenge, so I was definitely going to do the race. (There were Lululemon prizes involved, after all.) But I was not going to do it alone, so I enlisted the only two women I knew who were crazy enough to do this with me: Bekah and Annie. Both had been runners at the University of Minnesota, and they too did not shy away from a challenge.

Once the crew was assembled I went shopping for the shortest shorts I could find. When it became apparent that finding shorts in November in Minnesota was going to be an epic fail, I settled for the next best thing, which was a surefire win: little boys' superhero undies. You read that right; the three of us proceeded to run the streets of St. Paul donning stocking caps, sweatshirts, and nothing more than little boys' underwear with Superman, Batman, and the Green Lantern on them. We paraded down the snow-crusted streets to the sounds of honking and hollering. We were a show, no doubt, but we were too busy laughing to notice.

We took a picture to commemorate this awesome moment, but I should have known better than to stand darn near naked next to these two perfect specimens. Annie has the legs of a goddess, with that natural inner-thigh gap we all try to get by attempting workouts on Pinterest for a week until we give up because we haven't seen results yet. Bekah has the most beautifully muscular thighs I have ever seen on a woman (don't judge—you know we check each other out) and a rack that people pay good money for. Then there is me, a good four to eight inches shorter than both of them, legs like an overweight pony that haven't seen an inner-thigh gap since I was seven. I am thin, sure, but I have to work to stay that way, and don't even get me started on the board I call a chest. Needless to say I smile when I think of the memory, but that picture haunts me a little.

As you might have guessed, we won the contest and had a hell of a lot of fun. That's what I love about these two; they are always down for anything, not to mention they are my running inspirations.

Bekah is the closest thing I have ever had to a sister. I am the oldest, with two younger brothers, and while I love and adore my brothers, I've always wondered what it would be like to have a sister. Lucky for me we grew up in a very close extended family. I went to high school with my cousins, and every family trip I can remember they were there. Bekah is one of four, but there has always been something special between us. We can fight like sisters, push each other to the limit, and yet love the heck out of each other too. We have opened up to each other on our runs and exposed parts of ourselves that I am not sure we would have revealed had we not been physically exhausted and mentally on a high.

One of the things we have chatted about is my anxiety, her short bout with depression, and our family history of the two. To be honest, our conversation about it is part of the reason I decided to go public with my anxiety. We had the realization that no one is talking about it and how important it is that we do. We need to know that we are not the only ones feeling like this, that it is ok, that there is help, and that we are surrounded by people who understand.

The funny part to me about all of this is why the generations before us didn't try to help the younger ones cope with it. They had to see tendencies in their children, red flags that the anxiety was there. I see it in our kids, and already have them see my therapist from time to time as a way to give them tools to help combat the effects of something I know is in their blood. I am not blaming my mom for my anxiety, but I am not condoning the fact that no one is talking about it, either. I remember the first time I came home from the therapist and said to my mom, "She says I have anxiety." My mom said, "Oh, that makes sense. I have had it forever, and so do your aunts, uncles, and a few cousins."

I was pissed. How could she neglect to tell me about something I was so clearly predisposed to? Why is it that we are all dealing with it on the inside but not expressing it on the outside? Why do we feel the need to hide something beyond our control? Why the secrecy?

It angered me from the start, partially that I had anxiety and partially that no one was talking about it. I immediately went from feeling alone in that conversation to feeling like I had a lot of people that I could talk to if only I could get them to talk.

I feel as though the taboo around mental illness exists because there is no testing that can prove it to the world outside. No piece of paper with bar graphs and charts to indicate that your blood, saliva, spinal fluid, or urine confirms that your neurotransmitters are not functioning on all cylinders. It is just you, your word, and the people who choose to believe you. The skeptics will say that people are quick to go to a doctor to get a prescription for Xanax because they don't want to deal with the real world. While I am sure that happens, those of us living with these feelings can tell you it is way more complicated than that.

Do you ever stop to think that a predisposition to anxiety, coupled with the demands of a get-it-done-yesterday, I-need-it-now, let-me-return-this-email-immediately world, causes people to break? To me it is so apparent that the world we live in breeds stress, anxiety, and depression. How can we not be anxious when our email is constantly dinging, the kids are demanding, and work never stops? How can we not be depressed when everyone else's "perfect" life shows up on our Twitter and Instagram feeds, making us feel like we need more, want more, need to be better?

I am not saying that everyone has anxiety or depression. But we as a society put a lot of pressure on ourselves, take too much on. For those who are hardwired with mental illness, this can be the perfect recipe for a breakdown.

But enough of my rant . . . back to outrunning my genes.

> **"Let it go."**
> **–Elsa from _Frozen_**

...

PRINCESS HALF MARATHON

February 26, 2012

This race had been on my radar for a while. People had talked it up, making it out to be one of the must-run races, and so I drank the Kool-Aid and signed up for what I was sure was going to be one of my all-time favorite races.

The Disney Princess Half Marathon was far and away the biggest race I had been a part of to date. Because of Glen's job I had been given the opportunity to run races in some pretty cool destinations. Whenever the kids and I would travel with him, I would try to find a race in that city to experience a different location.

Up until that point, I had run most of my races in Minnesota, but got the chance to run the Princess Half Marathon at Disney World in the spring of 2012 while we were training in Fort Myers, barely three hours from Orlando. I have to admit that I was pretty excited about this race; after all, it was in Disney, and you got to run through the castle. But what I did not know was how early you had to get up, how many people would be there, and that you ran most of the course in the dark. Let me tell you, if you are a decent runner at all, this is not the race for you. You spend a good nine of the thirteen miles running alone through dark streets, the people behind you stopping every mile to take pictures with the characters.

This would be the first race that I would run with a bit of a philanthropic effort behind it. I come from a hockey family; the sport is in my blood. Although I have never played, I have been immersed in hockey since I was born. My parents had me young, and my dad was playing for Augsburg College at the time. So when I say since the day I was born, I mean it. In December of 2011 an incident occurred that rocked the state of hockey, involving Minnesota high school hockey player Jack Jablonski, who was hit in the middle of a game and was paralyzed instantly. Every hockey parent's worst fears took center stage as the whole community came together to support this young man. I, like so many who were thinking of their loved ones, couldn't help but think of my brothers. What if this had happened to them?

I wanted to do something to help. I started by convincing the Minnesota Twins Wives Organization to donate all our sales profits from shirts we were selling at TwinsFest in January to the Jack Jablonski Fund. But I wanted to do more. So when Lululemon at the Mall of America designed a one-of-a-kind #13 tank in Jack's honor and went to auction it off, I called and told them I would beat any bid. I decided to wear it proudly in Jack's honor at this race. I would run for him, because he would never run again.

So, here I was, rocking my white #13 tank out on the lonely, obscure, early-morning roads of Orlando. All that time along those dark and quiet roads gave me pause, and time to wrestle with a few demons. Being a woman alone in the dark does not sit well with me, never has. When I was in the heavy time of my anxiety, nights were the worst for me. Glen being on the road, me home with two kids, and the fact that his schedule was public information messed with my head. That people knew when there would not be a man in the house freaked me out. The slightest sound would send me into an all-out panic and sent my adrenaline through the roof. There were times when I would not fall asleep until three or four in the morning, conjuring up worst-case scenarios in my head. The only time I would get any sleep was when my mom slept over. Talk about anxiety that had spiraled out of control.

By the time I was alone on those dark streets of Disney I was medicated and therapy'd to a point where I was now able to sleep alone at night when Glen was gone. Maybe it was the meds or the therapy or the fact that we had moved a half mile down the street from my parents—I knew my dad could be at my house with a shotgun in thirty seconds—that put me at ease, but whatever the recipe, it was working. Thank God!

Having conquered the night terrors, I was now running down another demon: my baseball demon. You see, baseball has been a joy and a pain in our lives. It has taken us to the highest of highs and the lowest of lows. The lowest lows were something I needed to let go of. Glen was now back on the road to success in 2012, and yet I still couldn't shake my general negative feeling toward my husband's job.

Glen made the minor leagues look easy. He was an awesome starter right out of the gate. A number-one draft pick with high potential. For a while he met and exceeded that promise. He hit his first roadblock in Double-A New Britain, where he lost a little hope and spent a little too much time. Once past that point it was clear sailing to the big leagues.

He made his major-league debut at Fenway Park in 2006, in front of thousands of people and his seven-months-pregnant wife. He would finish that year in the big leagues, only to be sent back and forth between the minors and majors for the next few years. We had some good times in the big leagues during these years, and some bad.

The bad had left a sour taste in our mouth for the Twins, the fans, the media, and for people in general. When times get tough, you begin to weed out your genuine friends. We got a quick wake-up call as to whom ours were. We took what was said about us in the media too personally, me more so than Glen. It was around this time that I decided to stop reading anything about Glen, whether good or bad. This still holds true today. When it was all said and done, we were left barely standing, rattled, with a few close friends remaining, our hope intact but our faith in baseball shaken.

As I ran these streets in early 2012, we had moved past all of that, had gotten back on track, and back in people's good graces. This was not without a lot of work on our part, Glen's especially, and, of course, with a little help from the big man above.

Along those streets at the break of dawn I became ok with the fact that I may never be a typical baseball wife. I will never fit that mold. I deeply respect every woman who is in this life with me, for they are the only ones who will ever share how this feels. But I don't know that we will ever be best friends. Being ok with not being liked by all was a big deal for me. The people pleaser in me hated this idea, but I had to push through and find solace in just being me.

I have learned that this lifestyle causes me more stress than alleviation. I have learned that I am not as thick-skinned as I thought I was, and that I rattle easier than I anticipated. I am a bit of a worrier, a loner. When I think back to the girl who first came up to the big leagues with her husband, I see that I was overeager, a pleaser, and to be honest, probably a bit irritating. I quickly learned that I was trying to be someone I wasn't in order to impress people I wasn't even sure I wanted to be friends with. A couple years into the major leagues I took a step back and immediately my happiness returned. I felt more like me than I had in a long time.

Baseball is a funny thing. You are holed up by a contract, not by choice, with people you may or may not like. While it took a long time and a lot of soul-searching, I had found my balance, what worked for our family and my sanity.

Recently, with my therapist's help, I have also come to the realization that I am turning into an introvert, or maybe am just realizing I have always been one. This revelation surprised me. I have always been lively, involved, and outgoing, but in the last few years I felt like I was going through something. I could not quite put it into words, I couldn't explain what it was, but I knew something was shifting. I began to really enjoy my alone time, the time when it was just me out running on the road or writing. The quiet time that used to scare me I was now longing for. I worried I was depressed, worried that this need to have space made me seem distant to others. I came to find out I was just growing into my skin. I like to think I didn't change, I just found myself.

I have spent so long being the person I thought I was supposed to be: the perfect wife, perfect mother, perfect friend, perfect host. It wore me out. Being "on" all the time exhausted me to no end. I would go in and out of periods where I would be my old self, trying to be "perfect" and everything to everyone, then I would slip into who I was becoming and I would shut down and disconnect. It has been a hard transition for me, and one that I am still navigating today. I need to learn to put myself first, be who I am, and allow others to see the real me.

I worried for so long that if I was an introvert that meant I was a recluse. I now know that being an introvert means I am not mad, sad, or antisocial; it just means I need to be alone for a while and that's ok. I am friendly and enjoy being around others, but I need my downtime, too. Introverted people make their own energy, and rather than take it from others, they give it in social contexts. This means too much interaction can be exhausting, and they need time to recharge. I love my downtime, my nighttime, when the house is quiet and I don't have to think or talk. I need it desperately. Sometimes I shut down and don't talk to anyone for days. It is nothing personal. That is hard for people to understand, even me, but I am working through the adjustment and learning to be me.

The hardest part of all of this is learning to trust people with who I really am. For such a long time I have been a people pleaser. I wanted to be whatever people needed me to be in order to be liked. It was exhausting. Now, into my thirties and feeling more comfortable with who I am, I am ready to let that part of me go. I will always and forever be a considerate person, but I need to consider who I am, too. I need to let others see the real me, and hopefully they will understand. Hopefully they stick around.

And here along these Disney streets it was time to let go of what had happened before, the animosity, jealousy, anger, the pressure to be someone else. I was ready to shed that skin and find comfort in my own, in true Disney fashion. You need to be who you are. Others can take it or leave it, but at least you live a life you love and have no regrets. Can you even remember who you were before the world told you who to be? Find that person. Live in that way.

There must have been something cathartic about my thoughts along that run, because not only did I feel great, I ran great: 1:44:12, another PR.

"I didn't want to kiss you goodbye–that was the trouble–
I wanted to kiss you goodnight. And there's a lot of difference."
–Ernest Hemingway

...

GOLDY'S 10-MILE RACE

April 14, 2012

Spring was here, and so was my second year of running. Back to my alma mater for the first race I would repeat. I was excited to try it again, this time a little more seasoned and a little less nervous. Not only was I a better runner now, but I would have my college bestie Annie with me to help pass the miles as we tromped through our old stomping grounds.

Annie and I had met at freshman orientation before we even started at the U, and we loved each other instantly. She was my right-hand man, my partner in crime, and my shoulder to cry on for some of the most fun and fond years of my life. She is actually the reason I met Glen. Annie and Glen had known each other since freshman year, and when she would say she was going to hang out with Alisha, Glen thought she was making me up so she could blow him off.

The night I met Glen at Bobby Z's (a bar that no longer exists, which makes me feel old), I was a sophomore. I had ventured out that night thanks to Annie forcing my hand.

Actually, Glen and I had met once before our fateful night at Bobby Z's. Annie, yet again, had kidnapped me earlier that year to take me to a keg race the baseball team was having. She introduced Glen, and he proceeded to lay it on pretty thick—only to find out later that evening that I had a boyfriend at the time.

Glen, of course, does not remember this—guess that means the keg race was a success.

Anyhow, that night at Bobby Z's was one of the few times in my life that I did not have a boyfriend. I'd been trying to enjoy a few months as a single gal. I had gone on a date, if you can even call it that, with one of Glen's teammates, Tony. It ended up being purely platonic, and so that night at the bar with my roommate I was 100 percent a single gal.

Ironically, Glen was at the bar with Tony.

When we bumped into them and I was introduced, Glen said, "Alisha . . . like Tony's Alisha?"

To which I responded: "Oh no, no, no . . . no one's Alisha. Just Alisha."

We went on to connect the dots back to how I was the Alisha from freshman year, and I mentioned we had, in fact, met previously. Of course he did not remember.

All Rico Suave, he said to me: "Well, if Tony got to take you out, then I get to as well." Though this was rather cheesy, I did give him my number.

I do not think we have ever gone more than a day without talking to each other since.

We started as friends, the best of friends, and though I knew he wanted more, I was too busy being single, and I knew once I started dating him I would marry him. I finally gave in during May of our junior year, and we agreed to be a couple. He was drafted in June, and we were engaged by July. I told you I knew I would marry him.

There was a lot of history for Annie and me as we toed the starting line outside the new TCF football stadium, ready to run our past down. I have to admit I was a little nervous; Annie is an amazing runner, a gazelle, and I am more of a little pony trotting to keep up with her long, beautiful strides. She is one of those people who makes running look easy, and I think I make it look painful. This, coupled with the fact that I had not run outside since September, and I was in for a bumpy ride.

I am a wimpy winter runner. I feel like each year my blood gets thinner. Maybe it is all that time in Florida for spring training, or maybe I am just a wimp. Either way, I am a sissy when it comes to winter running. The first year I was a runner I wouldn't hit the treadmill until it was below 20 degrees; the next year I wouldn't run outside if it was below 30. As I write this, anything below 40 sends me indoors onto my treadmill to stay warm. See? I am a disgrace to Minnesota runners. Truth be told, I am not a person who hates the treadmill. In fact, I have grown to love my time spent going nowhere. It is my time to catch up on all the shows I DVR.

As many moms know, you don't get much time to yourself. The treadmill has become my bubble, the place where I get to zone out, get lost in my shows, and go nowhere while getting so much done. It is kind of perfection. I know most of you are cringing at this, but turn on a little *How to Get Away with Murder* and the miles will fly by . . . trust me.

So on that chilly April morning, I was going to give it the old college try (see what I did there?), brave the elements (and the gazelle's speed), and run with one of my favorite people. Annie and I love each other dearly but have gone down very different paths in life. I have been married for almost a decade, with two kids, and she is a single gal about town. We don't get to talk or see each other as much as we want, so at the race, as we caught up and reminisced, we made a pact to run this race together annually. I look forward to it every year and hope we are still running it when we are seventy.

With the gazelle's leg speed and banter, I managed to cut several minutes off my time from the year before: 1:29:20.

> "Let us run with perseverance the race marked out for us."
> —Hebrews 12:1

...

SNOQUALMIE HALF MARATHON

May 5, 2012

Three weeks after my second time at Goldy's 10 Mile, I was supposed to run the Lake Minnetonka Half Marathon. I had signed up months before but, as our life seems to go, something came up and we hit the road with Glen instead. Knowing that I was going to miss out on a race bummed me out, but I knew that the girls needed to be with their dad. Before we hopped on the plane to Seattle I did a little Internet digging and found a last-minute half marathon just outside Seattle in Snoqualmie.

When I signed up I had no idea what I was doing. I was desperate for a race (I was now a half-marathon junkie), and this seemed doable since the Minnesota Twins were in Seattle. I woke up early, left Glen and the kids still asleep at the hotel, and hopped into my rental car to drive the forty-five minutes outside the city to what everyone kept calling "God's country."

If you have never been to Seattle you must go. It is an incredible city surrounded by beautiful landscapes that make it unlike any city you have ever seen. I know it gets a bad rap because of the rain, but I have been there several times and have yet to see precipitation of any kind, so I am still in love. As beautiful as Seattle is, I was in for something even more stunning in Snoqualmie.

I pulled into the Snoqualmie High School parking lot and went inside the dingy, 1970s gym to get my number and stand in line for the restroom; I was sure the line would be long with the anxious last-minute pee-ers. To my surprise the line was short and the starting line was thin. A mere 485 people were running this race, as compared to the over 20,000 that lined up at the start of the Princess Half Marathon. I was a little intimidated by the small group, but was excited anyhow. The race began right outside the high school, where we headed on an out-and-back course through some of the most breathtaking landscapes I had ever seen. I was listening to a book on tape and was trying to focus on the reader, but was too busy getting lost in the scenery.

We ran through downtown Snoqualmie, with its cobblestone roads and antique-looking shops. The railroad tracks had such a patina that only a few specks of copper caught the sunlight and glittered from its rays. People were out rocking on their front-porch chairs, gliding back and forth, watching us go by. It made you never want to leave.

At one point I was running along a dirt road. To my right was a beautiful babbling brook surrounded by glistening river rock and tall, thin pine trees. To my left was a team of horses barely fenced in by old weather-worn fencing, grazing and running among the acres of field. Straight ahead was one of Washington's majestic snow-capped mountains. It was a moment that took my breath away and brought tears to my eyes as I thought about how amazing God's creation truly is.

To this day it remains far and away my favorite race. Something emotional happened for me there. I was able to fully get lost in the moment. My legs were going but my heart was elsewhere.

God is good.

I finished the race on the track of Snoqualmie High School in front of maybe fifty people. That is the thing about this race; it didn't have all the pomp and circumstance that others had, but it offered so much more. It had something the others didn't . . . it had heart. I hopped back into the rental car, encouraged and motivated.

As I drove I thanked God for allowing me to see the world through His eyes, something I never would have been able to do without baseball leading me there. And in that moment I was utterly thankful for baseball, a true 180 from how I had felt a few years earlier.

God has always been present in my life. I am a firm believer that God has everything under control. It is so much easier to believe that than to actually follow through with that belief, though—especially when things get rough.

I grew up in a Christian household. My parents were raised Catholic, and my family started off going to the same church they had gone to as kids. We did Sunday school, Communion, and church every Sunday like good Catholics do, but something was missing for me. I was a believer but did not necessarily want to know more.

This all changed in seventh grade when a friend took me to Hosanna! Lutheran Church in Lakeville, which had a middle-school program called "PowerLife." Ironically, the talk the pastor was administering that day was the sex talk, but nonetheless I fell in love. The music was fun, people were dancing, laughing, and smiling, and the pastor's speech was inspirational.

This was nothing like my Sunday school class at the Catholic Church. This was fun. I couldn't help but wonder: Could church actually be fun?

I went home that night with a newfound love and thirst for God and begged my parents to try church there. It wasn't a hard sell. They figured if Hosanna! was doing something that made a thirteen-year-old want to know more about God, they had to check it out.

We went as a family that following Sunday and were sold, even if my Catholic grandmother thought we were for sure going to hell. Pastor Bill Bohline is incredible. He started that church from nothing, and his charismatic teachings lead thousands to want a closer relationship with God. I am forever grateful for that man and the fire for God he lit in my heart.

As I write this, Bill has recently given his one-year retirement notice. It is with a heavy heart that I watch him move on to the next chapter in his life, but I know he is leaving me in the right place.

It is also because of Bill that Glen found a relationship with God. Glen grew up in a family that rarely went to church and did not talk much about God. Glen was a believer when we met, but his faith did not go much further; it was surface at best. I told him how important my faith was to me and that I wanted him to know what I knew. He was game.

Glen fully expected the Catholic experience he had grown up with from time to time, so when he got to Hosanna! and the music was pumping, he was a little thrown off—but also intrigued.

It wasn't until Bill started talking about Curt Schilling's bloody sock in the World Series that Glen realized he was in the right place. God works in mysterious ways. It was as if He brought that sermon to Bill's lips just for Glen to hear. That sermon made Glen want God in his life.

Glen got a strong dose of reality when stuck in Rochester, New York (the Twins' Triple-A affiliate). After a stint in the big leagues, he was down on his luck, his pitching was stagnant, and he was away from his family. With nowhere else to turn, he turned to God and asked Him to come into his life and change him for the better. From that point on he was a changed man. His pitching improved and his general attitude changed as well. He was back in Minnesota in no time, and from there on out he has been on the rise. I guess when life gets too hard to stand, you kneel.

I struggled early on with my faith and my anxiety. I felt like a bad Christian since I couldn't just let go and let God. I wanted total control, something I could never actually have but thought I could. I fought with these ideas in my mind, the condemning ones telling me that if I just believed in God then I shouldn't feel like this, I should just know He has everything under control.

I was told it was the devil trying to mess with me, trying to make me sin. I believed that, too, but thought that if I believed in Jesus then I should be able to overcome the anxiety. I shamed myself into submission. I degraded myself until I couldn't take it anymore. I threw up my hands and admitted this was nuts; there was more going on here, more than the bad guy trying to take me down.

I wish it were that easy to just let go and let God; man, do I ever. I spent a lot of time with my therapist (who is also a strong Christian) talking about this very thing, the shame I felt for the way I was wired. How could I claim to be a Christian and yet not have full faith in God's plan for me?

My answer to that is a simple one: I am a Christian but I am also human. Some people think that if you are a believer you don't sin, and that is so far from the truth.

The fact of the matter is that we all sin, we all wrestle with demons, and we all fail. The reason I am able to keep fighting, keep trying, is that I know God forgives me and wants the best for me. I know that I am not perfect. I will struggle—in fact, Jesus mentions in the Bible that there are going to be struggles in this imperfect world we live in—but what I also know is that I am trying.

I am trying to give up the illusion of control, trying to put every worry in God's hands, and trying to become a better person than I was the day before. I am trying to let my faith be bigger than my fears, and trying to be thankful for my struggle because without it I would have never found my strength.

Time: 1:48:16.

"If it is important, you will find a way.
If not, you will find an excuse."
-Unknown

...

GRANDMA'S HALF MARATHON

June 16, 2012

Just five weeks later it was time for Grandma's Marathon, an epic race in the state of Minnesota. Even if you aren't a runner, you have heard about this race if you live here. The race is held in Duluth, about two hours north of the Twin Cities, and is one of the flattest and most fun courses you can find. Many people run this race to qualify for the Boston Marathon or to improve their PR. The course zigzags along the shores of Lake Superior, zips you through the college campus where hundreds of drunk college students are cheering you on and offering you hot dogs and beer bongs, then finishes through the beautiful streets of downtown Duluth and up the only hill you will see.

The race takes place in one of the most beautiful months of Minnesota, the warm, early summer month of June. The snow is long gone and the sun is shimmering off the lake. The air is barely moist with humidity. The trees are green again, the flowers blooming, and as the clouds disappear, so does everyone's cabin fever.

While I was northbound, back in the Twin Cities Glen was now slowly inching into the Twins closer role, which kind of made me laugh. When I met Glen at the University of Minnesota, he was a starter and assumed he always would be. I remember one night, early on in our relationship, down in Quad Cities, Iowa (the Twins' Low-A affiliate), when I asked him how someone became a reliever—or even a closer. You have to understand, I was baseball illiterate.

I mean, seriously, I knew almost nothing about baseball.

I can remember attending one Twins game in my life at that point— the one when Kirby Puckett retired and rode around the Metrodome turf waving good-bye in a Corvette. Honestly, I didn't even know Glen was any good at baseball when we were in college.

Once, Glen took a coaching course just to be in the same class as me (love at first sight, he called it). One day, the professor came over to congratulate him on his performance over the weekend. I turned to him and said, "Wait, you are actually good at baseball?"

Mind you, he would come to class with a Snickers bar and a Coke every day and weighed a good twenty or so pounds more than he does now. I'm sure he will be thrilled I mentioned that, but it *is* the truth.

As you remember, I was raised in a hockey family, and being chubby does not bode well for a hockey player. Hockey players are generally in good shape, with tree trunks for legs.

Then here was this kid . . . charming, funny, and, yes, chubby. But he could throw the hell out of a baseball.

Glen told me relievers were usually starters who did not fare as well going as many innings; closers were relievers who were incredibly good at pitching one solid inning. Essentially, they were the big shot that came in to close the deal—to end the game.

I asked if he would ever become a closer.

He quickly responded with an emphatic "No!"

So now my "never-going-to-be-a-closer" husband was slowly becoming the Twins' go-to guy in the ninth inning, and the role suited him better than any I had seen him in before. We have always thought that he may have undiagnosed ADD, so it only made sense that he would thrive in a role where he could go all out for a short period of time. He can stay focused long enough to do the job well.

While Glen was closing games, I was racking up medals.

I took on Grandma's Half Marathon wholeheartedly. Duluth-bound with my cousin Bekah and her husband, Jeff, she was going to run the half as well, and he was competing in the elite division of the half. I had long heard about Grandma's Marathon and was excited to experience it for myself.

The only bummer was that it fell on Father's Day weekend that year, so we decided to head home after the race and not stay for the party that followed. (Epic fail on our part.) Before we blew off the party we enjoyed dinner the night before the race with Michael Rand (writer for the *Star Tribune*) and Tom Linnemann (aka John Sharman, all round crazy globetrotter).

Tom informed us over our carbo-load dinner at Pizza Luce that he was going to live-tweet his experience running the marathon, though he had done zero training. He was going to call it "Sharktrek 2012." Rand, on the other hand, had done the training and was going to try to kick ass at this race. This left me curious as to how their dynamic was going to play out on race day.

That next morning, as the summer sun was still in hiding and the darkness covered the roads, we rode the bus 13.1 miles back from the start. Rand and Tom rode another 13.1 miles, where Rand would actually run a marathon and Tom would live-tweet his own attempt.

I have to admit, this part of the race is a real bummer. Riding that bus for what feels like forever really screws with your mind. You are watching the miles and minutes tick by just thinking, "Wow, I have to run all the way back." Talk about trying to keep my anxiety in check. I was near a panic attack by the time we got to the start, but tried to keep my cool. Bekah and I warmed up (i.e., I did my fake leg swing) and found a spot to pee in the woods so we wouldn't have to fight the porta-potty crowds. You gotta do what you gotta do.

I ran my race, Bekah way ahead of me, and don't even get me started on how far ahead of us Jeff was. He later told us that he had had the shits and ran one of his worst races ever, even flicking off the cameraman before the finish line. But his sh*tty run trumps my very best any day.

On the other hand, Bekah and I ran great.

I finished in 1:46:02 and was in love with all the cheering and beer bongs (though I didn't partake—too many bad college memories) along the way. As for "Sharktrek 2012," I am happy to say that not only did Tom finish the race, but he finished under five hours and with a beer bong or two to boot. I am still waiting for his encore performance.

> "Food is the most abused anxiety drug.
> Exercise is the most underutilized antidepressant."
> –Unknown

...

COLOR RUN 5K

July 15, 2012

I am a sucker for a good gimmick run, and one month after the party that was Grandma's Half Marathon, I was ready for some more fun. Give me just about any good incentive to lace up and I am there. So when it was announced that the Color Run 5k was coming to Minnesota for the first time, it didn't take long for me to convince one of my best friends, Anna, to join me and put a little color back in our lives.

This race was happening at an interesting time for me. I had recently cut sugar of any kind (even fruit), dairy, and wheat out of my diet. Strange, I know, but I had my reasons.

Since having Lyla I had started getting sinus infections that were getting worse each year. I was getting them back to back with no relief. Before Lyla I had never had one in my life, and here I was living constantly with them. It finally got to the point where my ENT suggested surgery. While I was not the least bit excited about surgery, I was willing to do anything to make them stop.

I had the first surgery in November of 2011 and spent the next few days in bed while occasionally getting up to neti-pot blood and snot out of my nose (disgusting, I know). I was starting to feel better for the first time in years and was hopeful that this was the beginning of the end of sinus infections for me. (If you have never had one, be ever so thankful—they are horrific.)

I would be lying if I said I didn't enjoy the recovery phase. You get to take meds that make you all sleepy (and we know I love sleep), and everyone either dotes on you or leaves you alone. I remember when the kids were little I tried to think of a procedure I could have done just so that I could spend a couple days in bed and no one would think anything of it.

This surgery was too good to last, and before I knew it I was getting sinus infections again. I went back under the knife in January of 2012 for what we hoped would be the final solution to this whole messy and awful ordeal.

As dumb luck would have it, two surgeries in I was still getting frequent infections. Neither surgery had done the trick, and I was still suffering through back-to-back infections, which were now making my runs a struggle.

I was too tired and worn down to run, and this meant I was going crazy and driving Glen batty, too. Without my adrenaline and anxiety release I can become a real bear (which is putting it nicely). I felt I had exhausted all my options in the Western medical world and yet had no concrete answers as to why this kept happening. I was ready and willing to try anything else, so when my aunt mentioned to me that I should try a colonic, I was willing to give it a go.

For those of you who don't know what a colonic is, basically they stick a tube (about the size of a Magic Marker—remember the ones that smelled?) up your butt and flush warm water through your colon. The water flows out into a tube, where you can see what comes out. Sounds gross, yet mildly fascinating, right?

Glen and I have long been into doing ear candles every few months, partially because we think it is beneficial and partially because we like to see what comes out. So I was ready and willing to openly accept this intriguing yet disgusting challenge.

Well, I did it in early July, and instead of what you think would come out, there was a bunch of white, stringy-looking stuff . . . yeast. (Again, gross, I know, but I need to get my point across.)

Turns out you can develop excess yeast in your body by taking too many antibiotics, which I was certainly guilty of given the constant sinus infections. I ventured back to my aunt to find out what was next, which turned out to be a meeting with a naturopath.

Dr. Stephanie at Newbridge Clinic ran a bunch of blood work on me and found out that not only did I have excess yeast in my body but I was also allergic to all three dairy proteins: whey, casein, and lactose.

The plan was to go on an antiyeast diet, which consisted of no dairy, gluten, or sugar of any kind, including fruit. I would couple this with a cleanse to kill the existing yeast in the process. The cleanse would be killing the yeast while the diet would cut off its sugar supply; the two together would help tremendously.

I am not going to lie; for the first week or two I would have killed someone for a Twizzler. I did not realize how strong my sugar craving from the yeast was until I took it away. With time, the diet got easier, and I ended up losing ten pounds that I didn't even know I had to lose. (I might have even seen a hint of that inner-thigh gap.)

As far as dairy was concerned, I was to avoid it from there on out—it was obviously part of the problem. So I started the diet, and in the meantime I wanted to have the naturopath see our girls as well since they had been having stomach and bowel issues. As it would turn out, they both have gluten allergies.

This meant our entire diet was about to change in hopes that the girls' symptoms would dissipate: no more pizza, bread, pasta, or crackers unless they were gluten-free. And those are just the obvious gluten-containing items; don't forget things like soy sauce or some hand sanitizers. For the first time in my life I had to meticulously read labels and pay attention.

Thank God for Chipotle and their "no gluten" menu (minus their tortillas).

Lyla's symptoms were so strong that we had to have her tested for celiac, which lucky for us was negative. We spent the 2012 summer changing everything about the way we ate and what we ate. I hoped this would help all the ladies in our house be on the mend.

Who knew the answers to my sinuses could come from my butt?

This race would be my first since giving up all the inflammatory agents entering my body. I was curious to see how I would feel, but

I knew the true test wouldn't happen until I really got my legs under me and ran a half marathon on the new diet.

Anna and I made our way through the colorful powder flying all over the state fairgrounds and came out the other side much brighter than we started. She was new to running, barely more than a power walker, and I, on the other hand, had a little more experience under my belt, so I didn't think anything of taking a call while we were running. She just looked at me, mouth agape, and said, "Really?"

The one thing I did notice throughout the race was a change in my anxiety levels. My anxiety had jumped through the roof when I learned about all the lifestyle changes that I was about to undertake. Rerouting every eating plan will do that to a person. Having to put meticulous thought into everything that entered my kids' mouths or my own was exhausting. I had a new appreciation for the moms with kids who have anaphylactic allergies; I cannot imagine the anxiety that must cause.

While the anxiety was at an all-time high in the beginning, as the weeks went on and I started to feel better, the anxiety also decreased. I truly believe that there is a huge nutritional component to just about every ailment we experience in life. We have genetically altered what we grow so much, and put so many pesticides on everything, that now it is coming back to bite us . . . hard. The relief my girls and I have experienced by altering our diets has been lifechanging. My anxiety has decreased, my energy has risen, the girls' stomach issues have gone, and my sinus infections . . . I have had two in the last three years that were mainly brought on by outdoor allergens, which I am starting to control with the help of sublingual drops from an amazing allergy clinic in La Crosse, Wisconsin.

I actually stuck to this antiyeast diet for four months. By October of 2012, I had had two surgeries, seen an entire team of doctors at the Mayo Clinic, been on all the antibiotics known to man, and had no success.

Now, after a few butt cleanses, a body cleanse, a diet change, and no more dairy in my life I was finally feeling like myself again, and my sugar cravings had subsided. I was hopeful, and I was also a believer in the homeopathic route. As my dad always says, there is a place for everyone. We have had great success with cutting gluten and dairy from our lives thanks to our naturopath, but if I break my leg I am not going to see her—I am heading to a medical doctor.

I will be forever thankful for that very first butt cleaning. Glen has always told me he loves my butt, and now I do too. I am bringing booty back.

"You ain't cool unless you pee your pants."
-Billy Madison, *Billy Madison*

...

GOPHER TO BADGER HALF MARATHON

August 11, 2012

I was on such a streak of monthly races that I couldn't let August go by without a half marathon in the books. When nothing seemed to jive with my schedule I signed up for the Gopher to Badger Half. This race really did nothing for me in terms of ramping me up to run it, but nonetheless it was going to get me a checkmark next to the month of August.

The shtick was that you started the race in Minnesota and ended in Wisconsin. The states are just across the St. Croix River from each other, so you parked in Wisconsin and ventured across the bridge to the starting line.

To be honest, the course was pretty boring; the run is mainly along rural roads. But that is not what was most memorable about this race. At every race there is a complaint about the lack of restrooms, but this race took it to a whole different level.

Not only was there a lack of restrooms at the start, there were zero—yes, you read that right—zero restrooms along the course. This meant that while you spent the next 13.1 miles chugging water and sports drinks, there would be nowhere to relieve yourself. You either had an iron bladder or you peed your pants.

I was of the first category until mile 12, while crossing the bridge from Minnesota to Wisconsin; there at the state line I lost it.

I was peeing my pants.

It was kind of an embarrassingly cool moment. Embarrassing because I was peeing my pants but cool because this is what "real runners" do. You have all heard stories of the marathoners who peed or pooped on the go because they were going so fast and didn't want to waste time. Well, I was one of them now . . . except my reason was not time but lack of facilities (which is not nearly as cool).

My in-laws had come to watch me at this race, and as I breezed by them at the finish line I kept running straight into the St. Croix River. I am sure they thought I was just hot and wanted to cool off, but they would later find out I was rinsing urine off my legs!

There you have it: I was now an "official" runner. Time: 1:46:20.

I proceeded to share my story on Michael Rand's blog for the *Star Tribune*. That the wife of a local celebrity would admit to peeing her pants caught a few people off guard, but for those who had been following my blog, this honesty was run-of-the-mill stuff.

I had started my blog in January of 2012 with the intent to inspire, encourage, and compel others to get out there and run, or at the very least get active. I had hoped my honesty, sense of humor, and humility would make me seem approachable and make running seem attainable.

I had never written anything besides all those term papers in college. I like to hold that one over Glen's head because while he is better than me at a lot of things, I am the one with the degree. But now running had given me a voice I felt I needed to share. Call it God, call it divine intervention, call it what you want, but I felt compelled to write about my ups and downs while on this running journey. I know running can be scary and daunting, and those who call themselves runners are often so intimidating that those wanting to try it are scared they won't be as good. I am far and away not the fastest runner out there. (Remember the fat pony reference?) I pound the pavement like the rest of you, for the feeling, the high. I would love to make it look easy, to be able to win a race, but that is not me. I will never be the fastest or the strongest, but I try to be the most authentic and inspiring.

I also wanted to be able to share tips and suggestions for new runners from my experiences. One thing I've noticed in the running community is how many questions there are. Even seasoned veterans are asking others what they are doing to get better, faster, stronger, or just to get by. A lot of their knowledge and mine comes from trial and error, and maybe sharing my errors with you can help you get to your end goal quicker.

The even greater part about runners is that they all seem willing to share their knowledge. Running is not a one-size-fits-all activity. What you love and what works for you may be totally different than what works for others. Though I love and respect Bekah and her running knowledge dearly, we do butt heads on what the best shoes, gear, and fuel are, but that's the beauty in it.

we share our stories out of the mutual respect we all have for the fact that we're fitting in a run despite the balance of work and family, or maybe it is just that we need to feel connected. Either way, what is greatest about running is that it is always the same, yet always changing.

The questions I get asked most:

What's on my playlist? Truthfully quite an eclectic mix. Whatever is hip, recent, and up-tempo. Probably a book on tape.

What shoes do I run in? Well, I have run in just about all of them. I love Brooks shoes and my Adidas Energy Boosts, but as of recently I am deep in love with my Saucony Kinvaras. Their zero drop and wide toe box are huge pluses for me. Everyone's feet are different, though, so you should head to your local running store (ideally the folks at Mill City, if you happen to live in the Twin Cities) and have them watch you run. They'll then recommend shoes based on your individual feet for the best feel and fit.

What do you use for fuel during a race? I feel like I have tasted every drink, bar, and gel on the market. For a long time I used GU products, but when I started to get health conscious and wanted a more natural product I switched over to Hüma Chia Gels and I love them. They taste like fruit jellies, and they seem to give me a better kick than any of the overprocessed products do.

What watch do you use? Do you use a heart monitor? I have also dabbled quite a bit in the watch market. I've tried products by Nike, Garmin, and Bia. I used to always go back to my Garmin Forerunner 15; it seemed to have the most accurate data and connected to satellites easily, not to mention it was nice and small on my tiny wrists. But then I found the Garmin Vivoactive. It is Garmin's first attempt at a smart watch, and while the GPS connects crazy fast and the accuracy is awesome, I especially love seeing my number of steps during the day and the gentle vibration whenever I get a text. I am in love. I am not a heart monitor person, but it has that feature too. I keep a pretty consistent pace and know when I am taxing myself. I understand why people use heart monitors, but they aren't for me. I can barely handle wearing a watch, much less something around my ribcage.

What is your favorite clothing company to hit the pavement in? I am not sure that I have one answer to this. I like several things from many companies, but if I had to put together my favorite running outfit it would be my Mill City Running Fitsoks, my Lululemon speed shorts, a Nike padded sports bra, and a thin, lightweight, sweat-wicking tank from Nike or Lululemon.

I could probably go on and on giving advice on running dos and don'ts, but instead you should just check out the blog (www. alishaperkins.com) and shoot me any questions you want answered.

Now I was a runner and a writer, two distinctions I never imagined having, much less loving. And I was peeing my pants just to prove I was the real deal.

"Veronica and I are trying this new fad called, uh, jogging.
I believe it's jogging, or yogging. It might be a soft 'j.'
I'm not sure, but apparently you just run for an extended
period of time. It's supposed to be wild."
—Ron Burgundy, *Anchorman*

...

FIFTEEN'S 5K

August 12, 2012

After I had changed my pants, showered, and slept, it was time to get up and at 'em for the very first Fifteen's 5k. You'll remember that this race started as an idea I cooked up during one of my half marathons. I felt in my bones that this was going to be a good thing, something to make running fun for others.

You remember when running was fun, right? As a kid, when you would take off in a sprint for no reason whatsoever. The wind blowing through your hair as you played "boys chase girls" all around the playground. You never worried about how long you had to go or what speed you were running. You weren't training for anything, and you didn't want it to end. You could run forever because you loved to run, it was freeing, and it was how you got away.

It seemed that every game growing up involved running: chase, tag, red rover, kickball, and my all-time favorite, kick the can. Every summer night as a kid, right around dusk, all the kids in our neighborhood would don their dark clothes and head out to play in the street. Without a word spoken, no texting or calling, we would all show up and be ready to rumble.

For those of you unfamiliar with kick the can, the game is simple: it is essentially tag, hide and seek, and capture the flag rolled into one (which actually doesn't make it sound simple). One person is deemed "it" and there is a can or bucket placed in the middle of the street. The other players run off and hide as "it" counts. "It" then tries to find and tag each player. Once you are tagged you are sent to "jail" (usually a nearby driveway) while you wait for someone who hasn't been tagged to come and kick the can to free you. The catch is that, in order to free the prisoners, the person kicking the can also can't get tagged, so they have to be strategic and fast. I was both.

I loved this game. It allowed me to capitalize on my speed and be the hero. I can remember playing this for hours every warm summer night. I loved the thrill of sprinting out and saving the day. Maybe that was my first hit of the runner's high.

Can you imagine that happening now? Does anyone even play this anymore?

I, for one, cannot fathom allowing my kids to dress in all black and play in the center of the street in the middle of the night with little to no adult supervision. It sounds like my worst nightmare, and that saddens me. My kids will never know that feeling, being free from your parents' watchful eye and getting that first hit of a runner's high, of what it feels like to save the day. It is a different time now, and I hate that my kids lose out because of it.

So, on this day, the inaugural Fifteen's 5k, I was looking to give others their initial hit of a runner's high, their "kick the can" experience. I woke up at the butt crack of dawn and piled into my dad's truck for what was sure to be an exciting and exhausting day. (If only I liked coffee; it would be really convenient on days like this.)

The 5k run started near Gold Medal Park in Minneapolis, snaked its way through downtown, and ended outside Target Field. Glen and I called in just about every assist and favor we could to make it the best event possible. We brought in all the local mascots, Viking cheerleaders, and local radio stations, and capped the race off by having the Twins players hand medals to the runners.

Glen and I started the race the first year and then drove in my dad's truck back to the finish line to be there for the first finisher. We even gave the first male and female finishers four on-field batting-practice tickets, and the person who raised the most money on their individual account for CF was given a chance to throw out the first pitch at a Twins game. We were trying to entice people into the race in any way possible.

Ironically, in our inaugural year, the first male and female finishers were my cousin Bekah and her husband, Jeff, which was only fitting. The race went off without a hitch and seemed to be a huge success. The sun was shining, people were smiling while they jogged by, and I was having the time of my life. I had never been on the other side of the finish line; now I got the chance to be the one cheering. Which is ironic because something I have never told anyone is that I tried out to be a cheerleader in high school but didn't make it. I am not even sure why I did it; I never wanted to be one and didn't really like the cheerleaders. I think I did it because my mom was one and wanted me to do it too, not to mention it seemed like the boys gravitated toward those short pleated skirts. But I apparently wasn't spunky enough and got the ax. Don't tell anyone; I am still embarrassed by the whole ordeal.

I wanted to encourage and inspire people to finish strong, but instead they emboldened me. We had over 700 runners our first year, and each one brought me near tears. To see people coming together, families with little kids, people in wheelchairs, all out there running for something bigger than them was incredible. It gives me goose bumps even as I write about it.

I knew right then and there we had done something special, and there was no way we were going to stop. We raised over $18,000 for cystic fibrosis that first year.

God is good!

"She's whiskey in a teacup."
—Unknown

...

WOMEN ROCK HALF MARATHON

September 1, 2012

Coming off my high from Fifteen's 5k I found myself at the starting line for the first year of the Women Rock Half Marathon in Minnesota. I was keeping my once-a-month half-marathon streak intact with this race, and they had promised champagne and hot firemen at the end. Remember, I love me a good gimmick, and so I was in.

I had hoped to run this race with a friend in the spirit of girl power and camaraderie, but no such luck. Instead I spent the next 13.1 miles thinking about all the amazing women in my life. The ones who inspire me, teach me, touch me, love me, and support me.

I thought about my mom. The woman who has been with me through it all and still loves me the same. The woman who taught me to suck it up and keep going because that is what she did. The woman who always gives her opinion, even when not asked, and loves us so much that she can't let us go.

Jenna, my nanny and "little sister" for the last five years. She has been a role model for my children, one of the few people I fully trust with my kids. She is one of the kindest-hearted and most patient people I have ever met. It has been my honor to watch her grow into the amazing young woman she is.

Bekah, my cousin and "sister." By now you know I love her, and I could list a million reasons why, but most importantly she loves me in spite of me. She is my running guru, and I look up to her even though she is younger than me. She inspires me to be better, not only in running but in life.

Nicole, my person. She is the type of person that loves with her whole heart. Once you are in, she is fiercely loyal and so incredibly thoughtful. She makes me laugh all the time, and being with her has always been easy and fun. I swear I have a girl crush on her; she is my soul mate.

GeeGee, my better half. To meet GeeGee is to love her. She is a sweet southern belle with a drawl that makes everyone in Minnesota swoon, and a wit that makes you want to constantly be around her. I can never thank her enough for the effect that she has had on my life and my anxiety. GeeGee is my easygoing, no-plans, fly-by-the-seat-of-your-pants friend, and she has instilled some of that in me, which has helped me to let my guard down and relax. I love her to death.

Alyssa, my running partner. We have not talked about her yet in the book but we will get there, I promise. She was a godsend to me. I prayed for someone to run with, to pass the time with, and then suddenly she appeared. She and I are like two peas in a pod, and running with her is my favorite part of the week. She is spunky and smart and so sweet.

Anna, my longtime bestie. I have known Anna for about seven years now, and though we immediately hit it off, our love for one another seems to grow more and more each year. She blows me away with her intelligence and love. She is one of the most genuine people I have ever met. She holds those she loves so close, and I am honored to be one of those people in her life.

Meghann, my lifelong friend. I have known Meg since we were in elementary school. We grew up in the same town, and our families ran in the same circles. Meg is one of the kindest and most endearing people I have ever known. She is also one of the best moms I know. We have made it this far together, and I am sure there is no stopping this friendship now.

Mackenzie, the reacquainted one. Mackenzie and I also grew up in the same town and actually babysat for the same family. We were aware of one another but were never really friends when we were younger. We reconnected not too long ago, and I could not be more thrilled to have her in my life. She is one of the most generous and thoughtful people I know. She never forgets a birthday and is always offering to take the kids off my hands when Glen is on a long road trip. I admire her goodness and aspire to be the kind of friend she is.

There are obviously so many more women I could list, but those are my nearest and dearest, the ones in my inner circle. I keep my circle small and tight, but once you are in I'm all yours. My anxiety prevents trust and forces me to close ranks. I am a fierce friend once you are in, and the few times those friendships haven't gone the distance I have been devastated. I take a long, hard look at people before I invest. We are all running on borrowed time, and when we have given everything we can to our families, spouses, and work, we have little time left for fun. I want to make sure the people I spend that small amount of time with are well worth it.

Along those long miles I thought about my running inspirations, too . . . the women ones, anyway.

I thought about my Annie and her gazelle legs; Elizabeth—my cousin and Bekah's sister—and her determination to see how far running can take her (and she is crazy fast).

I also thought about Cindy, a woman I had met at Mill City Running, who had come to the Fifteen's 5k training runs. She was a self-admitted new runner but was eager to learn, and such a joy to be around. She went from being barely able to run a mile to running our 5k, and just recently completed her first half marathon. Her attitude is second to none. Just being around her makes you smile, and her drive to get better and learn is so captivating that it makes you remember why you started running.

Sure, there are lots of professional women runners I look up to, but I am more interested in the real people. The ones out there just trying to get better and hoping it pays off. The ones who never give up, and whose willpower inspires others. I want to be one of those people.

I hope that all the women in my life know they have played a part in helping me to become the woman and the runner I am, and I am grateful to each and every one of them.

I finished the race in 1:51:58. Not my greatest, but I will take the gratitude I felt along the way over the pace . . . for this race, anyway.

"Obsessed is the word the lazy use to describe the dedicated."
−Unknown

...

TWIN CITIES 10 MILE

October 7, 2012

Five half marathons and one 10 mile later, I toed the line that crisp, cool, early October morning, the trees glowing a million shades of red, orange, and yellow. The air was fresh smelling, as though it knew winter was on its way. The ground was still free of snow but was covered in leaves that made the most wonderful crunch as you ran over them.

With so many races clumped so close together I was a little nervous for the TC 10 Mile and what the next couple weeks would have in store. I had signed up for the race in the spring, when the registration first became available. Even though the race was put on by the same race organizer as Fifteen's 5k (Twin Cities in Motion), I still could not get a guaranteed entry; the race is that much of a high commodity. I had heard wonderful things about this race and knew it was a hard one to get into, so I entered the lottery ASAP. Around the time I learned I got in, things got a little messy.

Toward the end of the season, while Glen was on a flight with the team, I had received word that Glen's college pitching coach, Todd Oakes (T.O.), had been diagnosed with acute myeloid leukemia.

As soon as Glen landed and called me, I had to break the news. I will never forget hearing my husband sob on the other end of the line knowing there was nothing I could do and no way to get to him. He had a job to do and was several hundred miles away when I needed to be with him most.

T.O. was a second father to Glen. When Glen arrived at the University of Minnesota in 2001, he was a self-admitted spoiled brat with a bit of an arrogance problem. He credits T.O. (and head coach John Anderson) with his significant turnaround. Glen will be the first to tell you that he would not be the pitcher he is today without the tough love and teachings that both great men provided.

T.O. knew the pitcher Glen could become and was not about to let an attitude problem stand in the way. T.O. also was not going to put up with Glen's crap, and laid down the law right away: shape up or ship out. Glen definitely tested the boundaries, but in the end T.O. won out and made him the pitcher (if not the man) he is today.

The cancer news was devastating; we wanted to do whatever we could to help. We sent care packages, said prayers, and visited when we could, but we wanted to do more. Since there was nothing else I could do, I did what I do in any tough situation: I ran.

That September I teamed up with Team in Training, an organization that runs to raise money for the Leukemia & Lymphoma Society, and decided to run the Nike Women's Half in San Francisco that October for T.O. I got to work fund-raising right away, and because T.O. is such an incredible guy who is loved by all, I raised over $10,000 quite quickly. But first I had the Twin Cities 10 Mile to run.

I was a little hesitant when I signed up for the Nike Women's Half for T.O. because I was already signed up for the Twin Cities Half the first week of October. The Nike race was to be mid-October, and then I had also signed up with Annie to run the Monster Dash 10 Mile at the end of October. I had never run this many races in such a short span of time before and hoped my body would hold up.

As I ran by the gorgeous houses on Summit Avenue and down the banks of the Mississippi River, I tried to take in the beauty of this state that I get to call home. I watched the sun as it was rising over the water on this cool, early-morning run. The yellow and orange light brought the sky to life as the leaves crackled under my feet, and the wind smelled of bonfires and freshly carved pumpkins.

I took a deep breath in and realized this was all going to be ok. I needed to be thankful that I could run, that I was not sick. I needed to do this for T.O. and for all the others that couldn't. The Twin Cities 10 Mile turned out to be one of my all-time favorite races in Minnesota. If you can get in, it is a must-do. The course is spectacular, the season is just right, the trees are a sight to behold, and the capitol at the end tops it off. I left that race excited for the races ahead. It was the perfect starting point for what was going to be a busy couple of weeks.

Time: 1:18:57. Killed it.

"I don't want to be alone. I just want to be left alone."
–Audrey Hepburn

...

NIKE WOMEN'S HALF MARATHON

October 14, 2012

Just a week after the Twin Cities 10 Mile, the trip to San Francisco brought me out of my comfort zone.

I had been on many trips with Glen, the kids, and girlfriends before, but never fully on my own. Sure, there were other people from the Team in Training group, and they were nice enough, but I was looking forward to my time alone and did not make an effort to make friends.

In my efforts to be alone I didn't realize how incredibly lonely I would feel.

I found myself texting Glen while I ate sushi solo, and found reasons to call people while I was out shopping. I did enjoy my "me" time, but only in limited doses. (Note to self: ask my therapist what that says about me.)

Race day came quick, and I was quite nervous. Not only was this another large race (20,000+ participants), but the thought of the hills that San Francisco is known for scared me to death.

The race started at a pretty fast clip, and while I wanted to keep up, I also did not want to die out. I wanted T.O. and all the donors to be proud of me, so I tried to mix being a conservative runner with my competitive nature. I thought about T.O. a lot along the way.

I wanted to give the race my everything for him. While the race might be tough, what he was battling in that hospital room was much tougher. If he could do that, I could easily do this.

That thought was all well and good until mile 6, the mile I had been dreading. Until this point there were hills, sure, but nothing like miles 6 and 7.

You had to run uphill for an entire mile. I am not talking just any hill, either; I am talking a 45-degree climb for 5,280 feet. There was no way to train for that in Minnesota, so I had no idea what I was in for. I began by attacking the hill, head down, barreling through. This was effective for the first half mile, and then things got real dicey.

To add fuel to the fire, Team in Training had coaches positioned along the hill to run with you and encourage you. One of them had latched on to me and would not stop talking. While I knew this was supposed to be helping, all I wanted to do was strangle him. This reminded me of giving birth to my two kids. Both Glen and my mom were there with me at the hospital, and I told them that anything I said in that room could not be used against me later—whatever happened in this room stayed in this room. In between pushes, my mom was trying to fire encouraging words my way and I just lost it. "No more talking. Got it?" I yelled, and that was that. My mom, like this guy, was just trying to help, but in the moment she was driving me crazy instead.

I think my hill companion finally got the hint about three-quarters of the way up. After I threw some sideways shade at him and didn't participate in the conversation, he wished me luck and peeled off. As he did, I mentally committed to not walking at any point on the hill.

I am happy to admit that I did not walk, though I am sure what I was doing at the end of that hill was more of a shuffle than a run. Though the hills on the course were killer, I was feeling great. I like to think I was drawing strength from T.O.'s courage.

During that run I thought about T.O. and the other men in my life who had given me courage. I thought about my husband and best friend, Glen. He loves me in spite of me. He is my everything, and I fall more in love with him every day. He is an amazing father and husband. He puts up with my crazy and helps me navigate the wild paths of my mind. His talent blows me away, and his fearlessness leaves me in awe.

The hero in my life, my dad. The man who taught me the value of hard work and perseverance. He instilled in me courage and strength. He is one of the most thoughtful men I know, with a heart of gold under a tough exterior. He is the person I admire most in life.

My brother Aaron, our "Bear." He was the first sibling I ever knew, and the one I am closest to. He is the opposite of me in so many ways and inspires me to be more like him. He has always been the relaxed, fun one and I envy him for that. He has been there for me through it all, and our relationship grows stronger every day. He makes me want to take it down a notch, and for that I am grateful.

The fighter, my brother Luke. He was always the one nipping at my heels, and from the start I knew he was going to be intense in his pursuits. He is one of the most driven, smartest individuals I know. He blows me away with his creativity and wits. He makes me laugh with his quick one-liners and helps me whenever I am too technology illiterate to get something done. I have been honored to watch him grow into the amazing young man he is, and can't wait to see what is in store for him.

Kevin, my other "brother." He has taught me that love can extend past family lines. He is Glen's best friend and quickly became mine as well. He is one of the most thought-provoking and boundary-testing people I know, and I love him for it. He has loved my children as if they were his own. He has taught me what it means to be resilient and steadfast. Though miles and time may separate us, he is always in my heart.

Toward the end of the race, after the miles reflecting on these men, I had an epiphany. At the 12.5-mile mark there were signs directing the half marathoners to veer right to finish, and the full marathoners to the left to continue on. I was feeling so surprisingly good that for a brief moment I thought about veering left. I had never in my life run more than 13.1 miles, but in that moment I thought maybe I could. I had spent my life veering right, always following the rules and for a split second the idea of saying "F-it" and veering left really appealed to me. In the end I stayed cautious and veered right, but I realized I was finally ready to run a full marathon.

When I got back to the hotel I texted Bekah to set me up with a training schedule: 26.2, here I come! (For real, this time.)

Oh, and despite the hills, I kicked ass: 1:47:21.

VERY FIRST RACE:
GOLDY'S 10 MILE, 2011.

MONSTER DASH 5K, 2013.

PRINCESS HALF 2012.

ANNIE, BEKAH, AND I AT LULU-
LEMON'S HOT TODDIES RUN.

ANNA AND I AT COLOR
RUN 5K, 2012.

RUNNING
WITH THE
GIRLS IN THE
STROLLER.

NIKE WOMEN'S
HALF MARATHON
FOR T.O., 2012.

ANNIE AND I
MONSTER DASH

THE FAMILY, WATCHING
MY 2011 MONSTER DASH
HALF MARATHON.

ANNIE AND I GOLDYS
10 MILE 2013.

MINNEAPOLIS
MARATHON 2013.

ADDIE AND LYLA CHEERING ME ON AT THE MINNEAPOLIS MARATHON, 2013.

FIFTEEN'S 5K, 2013.

POST-MINNEAPOLIS MARATHON FOOT TATTOO.

FIRST TIME SEEING TRAVIS, 2013.

ANNA AND I, SEAWHEEZE HALF
MARATHON, 2013.

MEG, SARAH, AND I ON A 10-MILE
RUN THROUGH BOSTON, 2014.

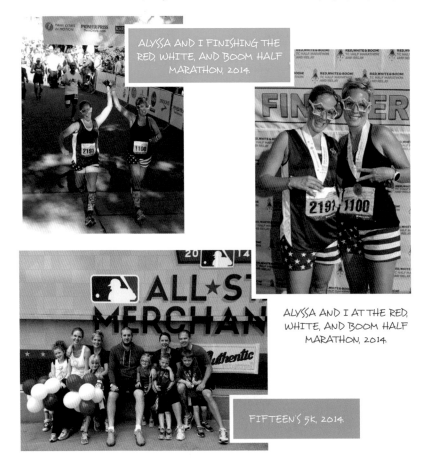

ALYSSA AND I FINISHING THE
RED, WHITE, AND BOOM HALF
MARATHON, 2014.

ALYSSA AND I AT THE RED,
WHITE, AND BOOM HALF
MARATHON, 2014.

FIFTEEN'S 5K, 2014

SEAWHEEZE HALF MARATHON, 2014.

ANNA AND I AT SEAWHEEZE
HALF MARATHON, 2014.

ADDIE RAN THE 2014
FIFTEEN'S 5K

TOUGH MUDDER 2014
WITH MY DAD AND
BROTHERS.

TOUGH MUDDER
MUD CRAWL, 2014.

TOUGH MUDDER
LOG CARRY, 2014.

OUR TOUGH MUDDER
FINISHERS' PICTURE.

RUNNING IN COSTA RICA, 2014.

MONSTER DASH
5K, 2014.

HOOTERS HALF MARATHON, 2015, WITH BECKY, JEFF, BEKAH, AND TRAVIS.

RUNNING PHOTO SHOOT WITH MY BROTHER, 2015.

"Can you tell me how to get to Sesame Street?"
–Joe Raposo, *Sesame Street* theme song

...

MONSTER DASH 10 MILE & 5K

October 21, 2012

A quick week later, I wasn't sure my legs were going to hold up. It had been an intense month, and here I was, finally at the end of my self-imposed race circuit. I was teaming up with Annie yet again, but instead of Goldy's 10 Mile we were going to take on the Monster Dash 10 Mile.

As you may remember, the last time I did the Monster Dash I ran the half. What they didn't tell the half marathoners was that at the 10-mile mark of the race you could literally see the 10-milers veer off and finish. It was so disheartening to watch them stop running, knowing you still had three miles left. (WTF, race director?) So this time I wised up and signed up for the ten mile instead of the half; the ten mile is my favorite distance anyway.

Annie and I are quite a pair. She is 5 feet 10, super thin, with long brown hair and beautiful brown eyes. I am all of 5 feet 2, with a thin but athletic build, short bleach-blonde hair, and bluish-green eyes. We could not be more different, so trying to come up with costumes for the race was a bit of a challenge.

In the end we toed the starting line as Big Bird and Cookie Monster; I will give you one guess as to who was who.

The ten miles flew by as we caught up and laughed. Being with her always makes me feel as free and easy as we were in college. (Not "easy" in that way . . .)

At the end of the race I left my college mentality for the real world, hopped into Glen's car, and drove like a bat out of hell across town to the Monster Dash 5k, where Anna was waiting with her kids and mine all dressed as crayons to run/walk the 5k. I will admit the two races were a lot to take on in one morning, but I wouldn't have missed either of them for the world.

I want my kids to like running, so I've tried to find ways to get them into it young. Monster Dash seemed to offer a winning combo: costumes, candy, medals, and the chance for the girls to hang with their besties. We probably did more walking than running, but I like to think the general idea came across.

I tried to relish the moment and enjoy the last of my running days outdoors, because if history tells us anything, I would be on the treadmill as soon as it hit 50 degrees.

Lucky for me, it is never too long on the treadmill before we head to Florida for spring training. Every year without fail we leave for Fort Myers in early February for Glen's season to begin. A bittersweet time, because while it is nice to be a family in the warm weather for two months, it also means that baseball season is beginning, and that soon, Glen is not going to be around for a while.

This spring training would have quite the running emphasis, more so than years prior. Florida will always have a special place in my heart: it is where I learned to run, where I learned to love the sound of my feet hitting the pavement, and the sound of my mind slowing down. I learned to love our time there, because I get to run, be outside, and be in the moment. This year would be no different, except this year I would be training for the long-awaited full marathon.

Bekah had come up with a plan for me to follow in order to achieve the full thing, the real deal. Pushing my body past its limits was something I wanted to experience.

It is funny how challenge intrigues me. You would think the opposite would be true, that the anxiety would keep me on the straight and narrow, not wanting to color outside the lines. Anxiety tells you that you can't feel uncomfortable, that things need to be a certain way, but there is a part of me that wants to feel uncomfortable, that wants to skirt the edges. I alluded to this in the beginning of the book—that what makes anxiety so hard for people to understand is that it manifests in different forms in different people.

How is it that a girl who can't sleep alone, who is terrified that someone is going to take her kids, and strives for control at every turn has no problem driving across the country with two kids in tow, or boarding several airplanes a month, and craves the out-of-control feeling you get on amusement-park rides?

That's the tricky part, the part that makes people question if it is all in your head. How can you do this but not that? I wish I had an answer, but the fact of the matter is that anxiety doesn't make sense, not even to those of us living with it. It is a beast and burden because you never know what will trigger your anxiety and what will release it.

My advice is to just live. Don't let your fear get in the way, and if it rears its ugly head, deal with it then. Talk to someone, see a therapist, take a damn pill, or run. There hasn't been a time when I hit the pavement that I didn't feel at least a little better after.

While I was outrunning my fears and chasing my marathon dreams, Bekah and Jeff came to Florida to visit us and were kind enough to join me on one of my long runs. This would turn out to be more than just a long run; this was the run where they let me in on their little secret, a secret that would change their lives forever. On a secluded path in Fort Myers, after being called "joggers" by a cop, much to Jeff's offense, they told me they were considering opening up their own running store. I was the first person they had run the idea by, and I could not have been more over the moon. I even offered to buy in, but to no avail.

Not too long after, they would get the keys to a gorgeous brick-laden building in Northeast Minneapolis, where they would open Mill City Running. The community rallied around the store immediately, partially due to the amazing owners and the effort they put into every customer interaction, but also due to the group runs they initiated, which encourage people of all running levels to bond and get out there. Similar to my goals with my blog, Bekah and Jeff wanted to make running attainable for anyone and everyone. There is no judgment whatsoever in that store, and they will be your biggest fans if you let them. The group runs give people a place to run and a purpose; it was a winning combination.

Even if you are not a runner, you *need* one of Mill City Running's amazing sweatshirts. Those sweatshirts are my safe place. The minute I put one on I know everything is going to be ok. That sweatshirt means it is time to relax and wind down. That sweatshirt, to me, is home.

I went so far off on a tangent that I almost forgot to tell you my time for the Monster Dash 10 Mile: 1:22:29.

> "The hardest step for a runner is the first one out the door."
> —Unknown

...

GOLDY'S 10 MILE RACE

April 13, 2013

Once back in Minnesota, as I entered my third year of running, Glen got right to work as the Twins' official closer, and things seemed to be going swimmingly for him. I was still training for my first full marathon but had suffered a minor setback. While training in Florida I developed piriformis syndrome, which means I pulled a muscle deep in my butt, and it hurt anytime I ran or sat.

I was diagnosed with a sluggish gluteus maximus, which affected my smaller piriformis muscle. Basically, the doctor told me I had a "lazy ass," which, of course, was far from the truth. I took some time off, got a few painful deep tissue massages, rolled my lazy ass on the lacrosse ball twice a day, and was back at it in no time.

Don't ever call me a lazy ass.

April 13 brought Goldy's Ten Mile with my college roomie Annie, but this time was different. My bestie, Anna (the similar names add confusion, I know, but hang in there), had decided that she wanted to run a half marathon, though she had never in her life run more than a mile. We signed up for Lululemon's SeaWheeze Half Marathon, taking place in August of 2013, and began her training a full year before.

Anna had no goals for the race other than to actually finish. While we could have enlisted Bekah's help to coach her along, I felt that since I had been working through Bekah's plan myself, and since Anna didn't want too much out of the race, I could be her coach. So now I was going to be a coach, which, to be fair, had been my minor in college, but I had never done anything with that knowledge until now.

Anna turned out to be a tough case. She is one of the busiest people I know, and her travel schedule is nuts. Trying to find time for her to get the workouts in was hard. We started with a four-times-a-week schedule, went down to three times a week, eventually down to two times, and ended with me begging her to at least get her long run in. I love her dearly, but she was a challenge to train.

Even so, she was moving me with her determination to accomplish this. This was Anna's "full marathon," and I did not take that lightly. I was near tears thanks to her inspiring attitude, but I am not a crier, never have been. I rarely let the waterworks fly.

Truth is, I want to be a crier. I want to be one of those women brought to tears by a Hallmark commercial or a wedding. It seems so feminine and pure to be able to experience emotion to the point where you just can't control it.

I blame the anxiety for my lack of emotion. Anxiety keeps my guard up just enough to not overthink the situation, for fear that I might break down. Fear: there it is, that word again. Fear is anxiety's biggest ally; it can hold you back with little to no logical explanation. If I keep emotions on the surface and don't allow myself to really take them in, really feel them, then I can't get hurt, I can't lose it. I stay stoic always, keep it together always, and never let emotions get too close to my heart. Anxiety tells me I can't handle it, so I don't. But I want to. I want to feel. As Hemingway says, "I want to bleed."

I have been married for ten years, and I can tell you that I love Glen more now than I did when we first got married. Not in that "growing old together so I have to say that" way, but in an honest-to-goodness truthful way. In the beginning I was scared to fully let him in, fully let him have my heart. I loved him, sure, but I always held back for fear that he would leave. I had no logical explanation for this fear; I was the kid of two happily married parents. But anxiety told me otherwise.

The question of "what if" is anxiety's other ally. Only in the last few years have I let Glen in fully, exposed myself to the nth degree, and allowed myself to feel complete and utter love. The kind of love that could crush me if he ever left, but which keeps me afloat every day. Making huge strides in my marriage led me to believe that someday I will be able to allow myself to feel something enough to cry. It has happened a time or two in the last few years, and while initially I was embarrassed, eventually I was freed, anxiety be damned. Let the tears flow.

Not quite crying from joy yet, Anna and I had gotten to work right away back in August of 2012 with our very first run together of a mile and a half, which included three bathroom stops, to the tune of sixteen minutes. We left from my house and got a half mile in before we had to stop for water and a potty. We then made it another half mile to the beach near my house, where again we needed to stop for a toilet. At this pace she was never going to make it through a half unless there was a porta potty every half mile—which we all know there is not (especially if it is organized by the Gopher to Badger race directors). We slowly progressed until she was keeping a pretty good ten- to twelve-minute-mile pace doing the ten-mile lakes run in Minneapolis, my favorite run in Minnesota.

The lakes run is one of the most populated trails in all of Minnesota. The loop consists of paved paths that go around Lake Harriet, Lake Calhoun, and Lake of the Isles, and motorized vehicles are restricted, so the run is quiet and peaceful. The houses that sit on the edge of the water are some of the prettiest houses you can find in the state. It is a safe trail, filled with lots of people no matter the time of day, and you get to take in some of the very best parts of the Land of 10,000 Lakes.

By the time Goldy's rolled around, Anna felt ready after nine months of training to try her luck at a ten-mile race. I promised that after my college roomie and I finished, I would run back to wherever Anna was and help her finish.

I ended up logging fourteen miles that day, but it was worth it to watch Anna finish. It was kind of a "proud momma" moment for me. There were no tears, but my heart was swelling as she crossed the finish line.

My time: 1:27:46 (and then four more miles after)
Anna's time: 1:58:34

Just for good measure I want to share another "real-deal runner" story with you. I was venturing out to run some intense hills, one of which my mom and I call Mt. MF. It was one of those beautiful early May days where the sun was shining and the outdoor running season had just begun after a long winter, so I was feeling good.

I got through my first three hills when I started to feel it: that pang in your lower stomach, the first signal that trouble is brewing. It quickly dissipated and I continued my hills. On the descent from hill five, things changed quickly. I was starting to feel the need to squeeze my butt cheeks together and pray. I was already halfway down the hill, so I decided to run up the sixth to get home as quickly as I could. I wanted to try my very best to get through all six hill circuits. While ascending Mt. MF for the last time, things went from bad to worse as I realized there was a chance I was not going to make it home.

Many runners reading this know the exact feeling. The moment where you no longer have control over your bowels, and if you don't squat now, you are going to have a messy-pants situation. I got as far as the woods across the field from the hill before the floodgates opened, and before I knew it, I was pooping in the woods. Mind you, this was early spring in Minnesota, so nothing had bloomed yet, which meant I had to clean off with crusty old leaves harvesting winter mold.

While weighing my options I heard a noise. As if this situation could not get any worse, I looked up to see that I was not far back from the parking lot of our local middle school, and the kids were being let out of school for the day. It occurred to me in this moment that if someone saw me I could end up on some sexual predator registry for dropping my pants at a school. So while I hid my face with one hand, I tried to pull my pants up with the other, which, of course, meant I did not wipe.

Lucky for me it squeaked out cleanly, but while I ran that three-quarters of a mile home, I couldn't help but laugh at the absurdity of what had just occurred.

Real runners poop. Really awesome ones poop in the woods, risk sexual predator charges, and still run home after.

"There is magic in the misery. Just ask any runner."
—Dean Karnazes

...

MINNEAPOLIS MARATHON

June 1, 2013

As you may recall, we have already been here. This was the date of my one and only full marathon, the day I checked it off my bucket list. This was an epic day for me, and one I won't soon forget. The training that led up to this day was intense. As anyone who has ever run a marathon will tell you, training pretty much takes over your life.

I was running a lot when the kids were at school, but sometimes would have to sneak in a run on the treadmill while they played on their iPads next to me. Training for a marathon is hard; being a mom and training for a marathon is even harder. Harder yet is being a mom with an absent hubby while training for a marathon. Tempo runs, strength runs, long runs, injuries . . . these all eventually led to me crossing a finish line I never thought I would reach.

You already know what happened that day, and while I love that story and would be happy to tell it again, let's instead chat about what happened after my feet stopped moving. I remember thinking a few feet before I crossed the finish line, "This is it? I just stop running? I have been doing this for four hours. How do I just stop?" Well, you do. It feels strange at first, but once you get your bearings you begin to assess the damage. Let me tell you, I was a train wreck.

The day after, I felt a bit of an emotional letdown, the same way you feel the day after your wedding. You work so hard, make so many plans, and it all comes together. The day is perfect and you want the feeling to last forever. Of course it doesn't, and the next day you experience the "what now?" feeling of the aftermath.

After I barely made it down the stairs the following morning, it became apparent that the marathon had left my body in pieces. There was the general soreness all over, the tattoo tenderness, the potential stress fracture in my left foot, and the uninterrupted sharp shooting pain in my right knee that had persisted over twenty-four of the twenty-six miles.

Quick time-out to tell you the funny story behind getting the tattoo. I have always loved tattoos. I like to think I would have sleeves if it weren't for my conservative husband. Still, I had convinced him to let me get a tattoo on my foot after I completed this illustrious goal. I had scheduled the tattoo to take place at 3 p.m. on the same day as the race, which gave me enough time to go home and take a nap after the run. (Me + sleep = bliss, remember?)

I arrived at Saint Sabrina's for my tattoo and was quickly escorted into the chair. After we got the design on my foot and I had ok'd it, the tattoo artist began. At this point I was exhausted and hurting from the marathon, so I didn't really flinch and may have even had my eyes closed. We lightly visited as he worked, and about halfway through the tattoo he stopped, turned to me, and said, "I have to ask, are you on something?" I honestly did not know what he was referring to until he clarified. "I don't mean to offend you, it's just that you seem so calm as I am doing this, and usually that is not the case." I informed him that the marathon he was tattooing onto my foot was the one that I had just run that very morning. He looked flabbergasted. "Oh! So we are working on no adrenaline here, huh? I will try to finish as quick as I can. You are a tough broad!" Twenty minutes and a drug accusation later, I was forever inked with my accomplishment.

Post-marathon I was a wreck, and what was a wreck to do but cram my aching body behind a steering wheel for six hours as the girls and I drove to Kansas City to spend the week with Glen.

To say I was stiff during that car ride would be an understatement; I was on the edge of becoming rigid.

Regardless, I made it, limped around Kansas City, and made it back to Minnesota in one piece. After a week of allowing every muscle in my body to slowly untangle, it became clear there was definitely something wrong with my left foot and right knee.

I had been prepared to not get out of the marathon unscathed, but I was hoping the damage would be minimal. I had planned to take two weeks off of running after the race, so instead of hitting the pavement I went to an orthopedic surgeon to figure out what was going on.

What I had not planned on was a hitch at the very end of my training that likely had something to do with my knee pain. On the morning of what was to be my final long run before the race, the inevitable

20-miler, it was pouring out, absolutely pissing rain. I tried to wait for it to let up, but when it became apparent that it wouldn't, I decided I'd better get my butt on the treadmill. Yep, I ran my last training run, twenty damn miles, on the treadmill. Thank God for the new Bond movies that I hadn't seen yet; without Daniel Craig, I am not sure I would have made it through. After that twenty miles my knee had started barking, but I did my best to rest up and ignore it, as there was nothing that was going to stop me from running that darn marathon.

Dr. Steubs confirmed there was no structural damage, which was both good and bad. Good because this meant no surgery, bad because the fix was not going to be easy or clear. He sent me to physical therapy, where I spent the next four weeks trying to fix what we could not even see.

The pain was real. I could not run more than 100 feet without shooting pain in my knee, not to mention my foot. We manipulated my body in a bunch of different ways; we used bands, iced the knee, and even ventured into iontophoresis, a process that delivers a medicine or other chemical through the skin, though these techniques brought little to no change.

My foot, as it turned out, was fine, but I had a subluxed cuboid that was causing all the pain. My physical therapist had repositioned the cuboid, and now it was on the mend. By the first week of July the foot was feeling a little better, but the knee situation had not changed, and I was beginning to get frustrated; the springer spaniel in me was ready to run again.

With no relief in sight, I was losing it a little and beginning to drive Glen crazy.

Though I was not able to run, others were, and these runners needed a place to get their running goodies. So on July 7, 2013, I ventured to Mill City Running's soft launch to check out the greatest running store of all time. (I may be slightly biased, but Yelp seems to agree with me.) This day, as it turned out, would be epic for several reasons, least of which would turn out to be the store's opening. (Sorry, Bekah and Jeff.)

I headed up to Minneapolis along with the girls and my mom to meet my brother Luke and his girlfriend, Kyri, with plans to check out the store and grab lunch along the St. Anthony Main area down by the banks of the Mississippi River—my second-favorite running area in Minnesota. Lyla had just learned to ride on two wheels and was eager to show off, so we hauled the bikes up to Minneapolis to ride across the Stone Arch Bridge, right down the street from Mill City.

Glen and I had already been given an early tour of Mill City before the launch, so I was familiar with the store, but to see it full of goodies and great people was so exciting. I was incredibly proud of Bekah and Jeff, and I knew good things were on their horizon.

While milling around (see what I did there?), I bumped into Travis McCathie—the guy my cousins refer to as "the Shaman" because they swear he can fix any running injury.

They had mentioned Travis before and kept telling me I should go to him, but having already seen a physical therapist and a chiropractor without success, I was sure there was nothing he could do.

But now here I was, face-to-face with the chosen one, so I bombarded him with questions.

He stunned me with his knowledge and wherewithal to even notice that the way I was standing showed I was favoring my right knee. After ten minutes with him I was finally willing to give it a shot. After we left the opening, arms full of the best sweatshirts around, I made a mental note to call his office ASAP. As we headed down the street and toward the bridge, my phone rang right before game time, which made me nervous. Glen never called before the game unless it was an emergency.

"I made it!" he said.

"What?" I responded.

"I made the All-Star team!" he said. "But you can't tell anyone until they announce it at 1 p.m."

I tried my best to contain my excitement, which was hard since I was walking with several people who knew it was out of the ordinary for Glen to be calling pregame. I could feel their eyes on me, wondering what was going on, and though I tried to be cool, I am a terrible liar. I can't keep a straight face when I talk to my kids about Santa. I was bursting at the seams to share this amazing news.

I quietly congratulated him and we hung up. I played it off by saying that the Twins' traveling secretary had a question about how many rooms we needed in NYC the following week.

We headed toward the bridge, with everyone enjoying the summer sun and me enjoying my little secret.

I counted the minutes until we were at lunch, along the banks of the river, enjoying our lazy-afternoon cocktails. When the clock struck 12:50 I couldn't wait anymore, so I spilled the beans.

"Hope you are all free next week, because we are headed to New York," I half shouted. "Glen made the All-Star team!"

Everyone was shocked and thrilled. We knew it was a possibility, but the chances were fifty-fifty. We cheers'd and celebrated, patiently waiting for the news to spread to the masses at 1 p.m. before we started texting others to share the joy.

By 1:30, both my phone and Glen's were exploding, and so were our hearts.

To think that only three years earlier we were wondering if he would ever play in the big leagues again, and now here we were, heading to the All-Star game in New York City.

I had just put a huge checkmark next to the "run a marathon" goal on my bucket list, and now my husband was about to check off his "make an All-Star game" goal. Hopefully he would get through his accomplishment without hurting a knee.

"Keep going! Keep going! (That's what she said.)"
–Unknown

...

FIFTEEN'S 5K & LULULEMON'S SEAWHEEZE HALF MARATHON

August 18, 2013

It had been two and a half months since I last ran, the run that had left my body in shambles. After chasing fireflies in Central Park, experiencing our first All-Star game and the hoopla that goes with it, and after my husband had gotten a save for the Minnesota Twins with his fly down (it's true—Google it), a full month had passed and it was time for the second year of Fifteen's 5k, this time with a big twist.

After 2012's race we had chatted about what a treat it would be for the runners if we could finish on Target Field. If only the Twins would let us.

Well, I took the idea straight to the top. In January of 2013, while at a teammate's wedding, I convinced Dave St. Peter to let us finish on the field. Maybe it was the liquid courage, but I like to think I picked the most opportune time to pose the question. Look at me, so business savvy.

With the help of a grounds crew that was thrilled, I am sure, we set up for what would be an amazing end to an already awesome race. We had doubled our registration numbers from the year prior, and geared up for a great day for a great cause. We saw a lot of family, friends, and repeat runners cross the finish line that day, and I again had the pleasure of cheering them on as they finished.

By the time the last person crossed the finish line, my hand was sore from high fives and I had lost my voice. But it was all worth it. People blew me away with their courage, perseverance, strength, and humility. It is funny to me how each year I pray so hard for everything to go well, only to see the stress fade. In the end, I'm just a girl standing on the baseball field, on the verge of tears, watching people fill my heart and inspire the daylights out of me. I hope we give these runners at least a tenth of the satisfaction that they give us.

Ultimately, though, it isn't about me. When the field was cleared, the runners with medals in hand, the players back in the locker room, and I was back in bed, we could all feel good that in only our second year we had doubled the funds for cystic fibrosis, raising $34,000. God is good.

While all these amazing runners were finishing their race on Target Field, where was I in the running world? Well, I had been seeing Travis for several weeks and was finally able to run a little. When I say a little, I mean very little . . . like a mile or less. It didn't matter to me, though. Being able to run at all was such a blessing. It had been ten run-less weeks (yes, I was going crazy and driving Glen nuts) when I hopped on a plane with Anna to Vancouver for Lululemon's SeaWheeze Half Marathon right after Fifteen's 5k.

As you might remember, we had signed up for this race an entire year earlier and had no idea I would be laid up when the big day arrived. I had been looking forward to this race for many reasons, largely because the course was going to be epic, and it was sponsored by Lululemon, after all. Since I could not run, the plan was for me to rent a bike, which I hate, since you don't get a runner's high with a bike, and you have to rely on a piece of equipment as opposed to just your body. I would meet Anna at a few spots along the course, run with her for a mile, then hop back on the bike and head to the next meet-up point.

The race start was unlike any I had ever seen. We got to the start literally fifteen minutes before the race began. We figured we would have time since Anna was in a later corral, but when we got there, not a single runner was in sight. I had a moment of panic, thinking we had missed it, since all the other races I had ever been to had people milling around and warming up at least thirty minutes before the race, with the elites usually there well before the commoners.

The start was a ghost town until five minutes before the race, when thousands of runners moseyed on over from the prerace yoga session. Leave it to Lululemon to make the whole thing so Zen.

I started Anna off and quickly deviated from the course to hop on the bike and meet her at mile 3, where fans, namely a few drag queens dressed to the nines, cheered on the runners with some of the funniest race signs I have ever seen.

"You have the eye of the tiger, and legs like Gisele!"

"You think this is bad? Growing out bangs, now that is tough."

The drag queens were the epitome of what made this race great. Lululemon brought out the fun, made you laugh, helped you forget the pain, and forced you to smile—hell, maybe even enjoy yourself. I caught Anna at mile 3 and ran with her until mile 5, which was the longest I had run since the marathon.

After getting lost biking through Stanley Park and going the wrong way out while the "real" bikers yelled at me, I caught Anna again at mile 8 or 9, and again for miles 11 to 12.5—where I ran ahead to snap pictures like crazy of my bestie finishing her very first half marathon. I was a proud little coach.

We spent the rest of our trip enjoying every aspect of Vancouver, which quickly became one of my favorite cities. When we weren't eating sushi, drinking sangria, or walking along their beautiful waterfront, we were cuddled in our beds watching HGTV and enjoying our kid-free moments.

Vancouver was perfection to us, and we did not think twice about immediately registering for next year's race. I promised myself that by then I would be running, not biking.

I was a runner again. Sure, I was coming back slowly, but I was coming back—and I had Travis to thank. He truly was a shaman—and might have saved my marriage!

"If you want to go fast, go alone.
If you want to go far, go together."
–African proverb

...

RED, WHITE AND BOOM HALF MARATHON

July 4, 2014

Yes, you read the date correctly; we are now over a year since the last time I crossed a finish line. So what happened to this one-time constant racer? Let's start at the beginning.

After those ten long, unrunable weeks following the marathon, I was finally (slowly) able to run without pain, thanks to Travis. It took a long time and a lot of patience (something God is still teaching me every day) to work back up to the runner I was before. The day after the marathon I remember thinking, "There is no way I would ever do this again." Wouldn't you know it, a mere six months later, once I was fully healed, I thought, "I should totally try to do that again, and get my time down."

I like to call this the "childbirth effect." In the moment you are hating every minute, cursing, and swearing up and down that you will never ever do this again. Give it a day or two and suddenly you have changed your tune. "It wasn't so bad. I could do that again." Crazy how the mind works.

So during spring training of 2014, healed and hungry, I set off to train for another marathon. I had somehow forgotten about the debacle that was the last marathon and had convinced myself to do it again—this time in an attempt to qualify for Boston, though it was a long shot.

I had planned to run the same marathon again, figuring I would stick with what I knew. Since I knew the course, the training, and the grind, I would be better equipped to run the race. No excuses this time, no knee injuries, just better results.

I had begun training after the first of the year and did a lot of running on the treadmill until we got to Florida. Though I had not run a race since the marathon, I had worked my way up in miles and was already able to run ten with no problems.

In Florida, away from the treadmill, I was increasing my mileage. All seemed to be going well. I logged eleven miles on my long run, twelve the next week, thirteen, then fourteen, followed by fifteen. At the sixteen-mile mark something changed.

I had been seeing Travis and a NUCCA chiropractor for a while to ward off the sinus infections and running injuries, but in Florida I was on my own. I prayed my body would hold itself together without the team that had been keeping me in one piece.

Along the sixteen-mile run I felt it: my neck went out of alignment early on in the run, and I kept going, hoping I was wrong. But by the end it was clear: my right knee was killing me again, and my calves were like rocks. It was a sad trot home as I came to the conclusion that I may not be able to run another marathon. I didn't know if that was something this body was meant to do.

It baffles me how people twice and sometimes three times my age can just whip out a marathon a month like it is no big thing. I truly think our bodies were made to run, but some are more equipped than others to run longer distances.

Take Dean Karnazes, for example. That man is a freak of nature, running the distances he does. Two hundred miles without stopping—that defies nature. There is no logical explanation for why he doesn't get hurt. Scientifically, he should not be able to do it. In fact, they say humans were not meant to run more than twenty miles— which is why a marathon is such a big deal. You are pushing your body past its natural limit.

It looked like my limit might be one and done, and I was disheartened. I needed something to run for; I wasn't into it on my own. I needed a race, a reason, or a partner.

In my many conversations with people about running, they kept mentioning their running partner. I was kind of jealous. At first I didn't want someone to run with; I liked the quiet time and the fact that I didn't have to fight pace with someone, but over time I realized why people run together.

In the beginning, running is new and exciting. You are feeling the high and jonesing for the next time you can lace up your sneakers and get out there. Over time, though, reality sets in, and running becomes monotonous. You simply put one foot in front of the other, distract yourself with the latest playlist or book on tape (if you are a dork like me), and try to enjoy the endorphins.

But the truth is, running is boring. There, I said it.

I will admit that I do love running, but at times I do it because I know I need to—not because I want to. In those moments it would be nice to have someone to get me out the door. I had belonged to a short-term running group consisting of me, Jeff Metzdorff, and Michael Rand (remember him from Grandma's?). We ran together two or three times, around the lakes in Minneapolis. We called ourselves CSE, which stood for Cushy Sock Enthusiasts. Sometime during those miles we had all discovered our mutual fondness for new running socks, and the rest is history. Unfortunately our history was short-lived; to be honest, those guys were too fast for me anyway.

My cousin Bekah was too fast also, though she was willing to dumb the pace down for me. Travis wanted to run way too long and always wanted me to run trails, which freaked me out. I am not sure exactly what it was about trail running that gave me pause, maybe it was the fear of getting hurt, getting lost, running into a strange animal, or maybe it was that deep down I knew I just may fall in love it. Anna was too slow (sorry, Anna); Annie, though I love her, was too flaky. I needed someone I had not even met yet, but I didn't know where to look. Craigslist?

Wanted: Someone to run with and be my friend. Must be able to run 8:30 miles and hold an engaging conversation. Oh, and please be able to run during school hours. No creepy men need apply.

Seriously, what was a girl to do?

As my dream of running a second marathon died, my desire to find someone to run with flourished.

And that was when I found her.

Yes, you heard that right, I did find a running partner, my very own friend with (running) benefits. I was so happy that I nearly changed my Facebook status. I bet you want to know who she is, right?

Well, her name is Alyssa and we met at Lyla's soccer game.

I usually make quite an effort to keep to myself at my kids' events, because once people realize who you are married to, things can get weird. People get awkward. So it was destiny that I met her. We were on the sidelines at the girls' practice when she overheard me talking to Addie. Alyssa asked which school the girls attended, and we chatted for the rest of the practice.

I felt a connection with her instantly.

That night I sought her out on the soccer email list (stalker-ish, I am aware) and suggested we grab coffee. To put this in context, you have to understand how guarded I am. It usually takes me awhile to get comfortable with someone and to make sure they like me for me and not just because of who my husband is. But there was something about her that made me trust her right away. We were similar (crazy similar, we would later find out), and I think that is what drew me to her.

Anyway, the signature of my email included my website, www. alishaperkins.com, and after getting my email Alyssa proceeded to check out my blog.

When Alyssa wrote back, she mentioned the blog and said she ran at about my pace. We agreed to try a run together.

The first time, we ran with another girl some friends had recommended, which turned out to be a mess; she was crazy fast and kicked our ass over four miles. Alyssa and I texted afterward and agreed we would definitely run together again—but this time without the other gal in tow (or in the lead, actually).

We met a few more times whenever we could, and I loved every minute of it. I finally had my counterpart. We have a similar pace and ability, and she keeps me entertained as we log the miles together.

We decided to run a race on July 4 called Red, White and Boom, which was put on by the same race organizer as Fifteen's 5k, Twin Cities in Motion. This was going to be my first race since I busted out 26.2 (and busted up my knee), and I couldn't think of a better way to reenter the race world than with my new running partner.

It was love at first gait.

On the day of the race, Alyssa and I piled into the car, hit Starbucks (I'm an addict, remember?), and headed to Minneapolis for our first race together—my running partner and I. (I just love saying that.)

We were decked head to toe in red, white, and blue, ready to celebrate America's freedom along the 13.1-mile course. The race started and finished at the Stone Arch Bridge.

As we toed the starting line, little did I know what a big deal this day and the next would be. I was oblivious, ready to start racing again. The next thirteen miles brought me joy, love, and a hunger for running.

Alyssa and I chatted the entire time, sharing stories in between each of us telling the other to slow down; neither of us had raced in a long time, and we did not want to die along the way. We finished the race hand in hand at 1:52:57. Not too shabby for two gals killing time chatting while their legs did the work.

Unfortunately, our good luck would not last forever.

Soon after that race Alyssa got a stress fracture in her pelvis and would not be able to run for months. As I write this, in early 2015, she is back in the saddle and running again. I am beyond thrilled and cannot wait for many more years of chat-filled runs. She was, after all, an answer to my prayers (and my imaginary Craigslist ad).

After the race and fireworks, the morning of July 5 started the same as any other, until Glen joined us for a family get-together after his game. There, in the driveway of my parents' house, Glen told me that he had yet again made the All-Star team—this time in his hometown.

He was excited to play in front of his fans. Glen was once one of those very fans himself, sitting in the Metrodome seats as a kid, cheering on his Twins. I couldn't wait to see what was in store. We both had been so blessed, first me with my answered prayer of a running partner, and now him with yet another All-Star nod.

God is good.

> "If it is both terrifying and amazing,
> then you should definitely pursue it."
> –Erada

...

TOUGH MUDDER

July 20, 2014

Just three weeks after being back in the running world I decided to test my limits again. I won't bore you with all the details of what happened at the All-Star game—this is a running book, after all—but in order to understand how we felt on July 20 you need to know what took place during that game.

After a party with family and friends at our favorite burger place, The Nook, Glen took the mound the next day in the ninth inning to try and earn the save for the American League in our very own home state. My stomach was in full knots, my mind was racing yet blank, and my heart was going a mile a minute. I was trying to remember to breathe. I cannot even imagine what was going through Glen's mind.

With my body and mind in a twist, I laid my head on my dad's shoulder, said a prayer, and watched as in the top of the ninth the bullpen door swung open and out ran my husband, the closer in the All-Star game at his home field. The fans had already brought us to tears (yes, me too) with their love and support during the parade, and they did not disappoint when he started his jog out to the mound. The place was electric.

Nine pitches later and he had retired the side in order. No drama, just smooth, cool, calm, confident Glen taking care of business in front of the most intense crowd of his life, on the biggest stage he had ever seen. He had just closed the All-Star game, the man they said was too arrogant to make it, too immature to succeed. If this wasn't full circle, I don't know what is.

As I thanked God for all the trials and tribulations that had brought us to this moment, I started to convulsively bawl. Lyla and Addie embraced me, and for the next ten minutes, as I watched Glen high-five his teammates, get swarmed by press, and hear the fans scream his name, I cried.

I let out four years of heartache and triumph, pain and pleasure. I allowed myself to just feel, to just be in the moment—a moment I could never have imagined in my wildest dreams. In that moment everything was worth it; in that moment it became incredibly clear God had the most amazing plan all along. I am not sure we would have appreciated this win the same way had we not gone from the bottom to the very top.

I let go of the anxiety and just cried. I didn't think, I just felt. Once I pulled myself together and took a look around, I realized the whole thing was pretty badass. My husband was badass.

With adrenaline still coursing through our veins, my dad, brothers, and I headed for the mound, too—the huge mound of dirt in Hudson, Wisconsin, called the Tough Mudder.

We had talked about doing this run for a few years, and it finally panned out. My brother Bear even drove from a bachelor party in Duluth, slightly hungover, to barrel through some challenging obstacles with Team Charros (a name inspired by *Eastbound & Down*). We had heard the horror stories about this race, but something about it intrigued all of us.

Waiting in a hot corral to start the race, we were pumped up by the resident cheerleader. It was a typical late-July early afternoon, and the sun was letting us know it was out for blood. The humidity, coupled with the sweaty bodies all around us, was enough to make anyone want to pass out.

We started the race at a decent clip, only slowing down after Bear threw up a little in his mouth, which was maybe to be expected.

We didn't run too far before we hit the first obstacle, where we had to crawl through mud under barbed wire. God forbid you arch your back or you were going to have a nasty scar. (How many of you are now hearing Taylor Swift's "Blank Space" in your head?)

From there we were back on our feet until we hit the Mud Mile, where we spent the next 100 yards climbing up seven-foot mud hills, just to slide down into four feet of muddy water and repeat. Once fully covered in mud, we ran to what I thought was the worst obstacle of all: the Arctic Enema.

Not knowing what we were in for, Bear and I went first. We climbed up the side of a wooden twenty-five-foot-long, ten-foot-wide, four-foot-deep hot-tub-looking thing—only it was not a hot tub. Nope, it was a tub full of freezing water that was filled with ice every half hour.

The water in the tub had to be colder than 40 degrees, and was muddy from all those who went before us. To make matters worse, we had to go under this bone-chilling water, swim under a wall, and climb out the other side. Did I mention the sign at the beginning of the obstacle? It read: *Keep moving. Risk of hypothermia.*

That kind of cold hitting your skin activates your flight or fight response and you need to decided which it will be and quick. We spent the next fifteen minutes after the ice bath running, trying to regain feeling in our bodies, while all the males were waiting for their balls to drop again.

The next obstacle was a twenty-foot jump off a plank into mucky water. This one didn't sound or look too bad until you were on the plank looking down, realizing you had no choice but to jump. Hopefully the guys' balls had dropped back down; otherwise their balls were about to be in their throats.

From there we had to work as a team to get each other over walls that were angled back at us like razor blades. This was followed by another team activity where we all had to get up over a thirty-foot wall using ropes.

At this point in the race my mom was supposed to be meeting us to get a few pictures as we conquered these crazy obstacles, so every time we arrived at another spot we would look for her, but never saw her. We would come to find out at the end of the race that our photographer had been too wrapped up at the beer gardens near the finish line to come and find us. It must be a tough life she lives.

While Nana was throwing them back, we were moving forward, on to monkey bars and rings over mud. Some of us made it and some didn't. I won't name names.

Down the final stretch was the Log Carry and Mt. Everest, where we had to run up a fifteen-foot curved wall and grab our teammate's hand before we fell. Finally we were at the end, with one crowning obstacle in our way: the Electric Shock Field.

Picture a bunch of hay bales underfoot, muddy water, no clear path, and above you, hanging a foot from the bales, are hundreds of live wires pumping out different levels of electricity. Just beyond are the finish line and that beer you worked so hard for. (I only wish I liked beer. My life would be so much easier if I did.)

You have two options in this scenario: you can get on your hands and knees and try to crawl strategically under all the wires through the mud and hay, or you can run like hell and pray the shocks don't knock you out.

We watched as people ran through and got knocked out, only to wind up face down in the mud and hay. At this point in the race we were spent: ten miles, ten obstacles, no puke (outside our mouths, anyway), and dirt in places dirt should never be, mixed in with blood and sweat. Needless to say we were ready to be done, so we ran like hell.

At one point, the shock hit Bear so hard he fell into me and knocked me into more wires. Lucky me. We made it out conscious but jolted.

I know it sounds crazy, but it was a blast. We bonded over those miles and challenges. If you have the guts, I highly recommend a

Tough Mudder. We were a little worse for the wear the next day, but the fun outweighed the pain in spades.

I come from a close-knit family. I am not even talking about just the five of us in my immediate family, either; I am also talking about all the cousins and aunts and uncles I grew up with. Glen always jokes that everyone in Lakeville is somehow related, because every story I have trails back to my cousins and how we all grew up about a mile or two apart.

My parents have always been my closest friends. Growing up, my friends thought it was strange how close we were, and even as an adult I have taken flack for the fact that my mom is always with us. But the fact of the matter is that no one knows me like they do, or loves me like they do. There is not a thing in this world I wouldn't do for them, and I know no matter what happens, they have my back. I hope Glen and I are half the parents they are. (They are pretty stellar grandparents, too.)

God knew I would not do well with a sister. I love our girls and am so glad that God did not give me boys, because I would take the drama over the chaos any day, but I am not even close to being a drama girl. I never had a lot of really close girlfriends growing up. I was always a tomboy, and girl issues drove me crazy. This is not to say that I didn't put my parents through the hormonal ringer as a teen, because I did. But outside of myself I couldn't handle it. So instead God blessed me with two amazing brothers.

We definitely had sibling rivalry and drove each other nuts, but they were also my favorite playmates and would fight to the death for me. I am the big sister, which means I was sometimes a little too mothering for them, but they loved me in spite of it. I don't know that I can put into words how much I love and admire them. They push me to be a better person and teach me things every day.

My childhood was very normal; boring, even. No divorces or big disputes. No surprises and no big challenges. To be honest, there were times when I wanted some drama, some story to tell others. Of course, I am thankful now that my upbringing was so run-of-the-mill. There were no significant highs or lows. I pretty much lived my life in the middle.

My family loves me through my crazy, and for that I am forever grateful. It is nice to know when things get tough and your mind goes nuts that you have amazing people on your side. It is such an incredible feeling to know my parents love Glen as their own, and to know that my girls are surrounded with the most wonderful support system anyone could ask for, people who will even run through live electrical wire for you.

I have no idea how long the race took us. The time doesn't really matter. This one was just about survival.

"I run because long after the footprints fade away, maybe I will have inspired a few to reject the easy path, hit the trails, put one foot in front of the other, and come to the same conclusion I did: I run because it always takes me where I want to go."
–Dean Karnazes

...

FIFTEEN'S 5K

August 17, 2014

We were kicking off the third year of Fifteen's 5k. Again we lucked out with the weather, had a few more runners than the year before, and I was incredibly moved by everyone's passion and determination.

There is so much work that goes into this race, especially on my part. You all know my darling hubby just shows up and lends his name to the event, though I'm ok pimping his name out. To see it all come together, everyone smiling, having fun, and making a difference makes it all worth it.

This year was especially extraordinary, because for the first time since we started the race, our girls got to be involved. Up until this point they were too little and too much work to keep an eye on as we ran around like crazy at the race. This year, though, while Lyla helped me cheer on the runners, Addie was one of them.

She ran the race with her bestie, Bree. Seeing her round the corner into the stadium made my heart leap. She was smiling ear to ear and having the time of her life. She was getting to be a part of making a difference in people's lives, running just like her mom. She looked so happy, and I was a grinning fool.

I try every year after the race—whether on my blog or by guest blogging—to put into words what this race means to me. Every year I fall short. No matter what I say, it will never truly explain how incredible that day is for our family and how much it means to us. I look forward to many more years of getting people to run, and watching those people change the world with each step.

We raised over $40,000 in 2014, and I hope that number climbs each year until we no longer have to raise funds for cystic fibrosis because there is a cure. I suppose we will then find another cause and keep running, because it is good for the soul and good for the soles.

I had now checked off my first race since the marathon mess and was back in the full swing of running. I had a couple other races on the docket, and while I was down a running partner, I was gaining lots of time for long runs and thought processing.

Our kids were both heading off to school full time, which was quite an adjustment for me and Glen. We had to figure out how to be home alone without them—and alone with each other.

With the kids back to school, what were we to do?

I know what some of you are thinking, and you should get your mind out of the gutter; besides, you can only do that so many times in a week. Even if we did, how were we going to spend the other seven hours and forty-five minutes a day that the kids were in school?

Granted, Glen was still heading to the field every day, but it was a new situation for both of us. I felt slightly worthless, which I hadn't felt since we first got married, when I had given up everything to follow him around the country.

What was I to do with myself all day if I wasn't being needed by my kids?

Never mind the being alone part. How was I supposed to trust someone else to be in charge of my little angels all day? I was sure I was the only one who could care for them in the way that they needed to be cared for.

How was I supposed to just drop them off at the door and assume they would be safe and loved without my ever-present watchful eye? This was a huge internal struggle for me, and it took its toll.

I would conjure up the worst-case scenarios: school shootings, bombings, bullying. I would be lying if I said there was not a time or two where I considered homeschooling, just to be able to have them close. My degree was in elementary education after all, so I could do it; the question was whether the girls would actually listen to me. In the end I sent them to school. They needed the social aspect whether I liked it or not.

I am sure many moms go through this very struggle each year. How do you let someone else help raise your babies? How do you know they have your kids' best interests in mind? That they will watch over them the same way you do? It is one of the hardest things a mom has to do.

Anxiety told me I needed to protect them from anything and everything that might come at them; I needed to be in control. Here I was trying to relinquish that control. I know I need to let them grow and make their own mistakes but anxiety tells me that I need to prevent any and everything bad they could encounter. It was gut-wrenching and sent me back to my therapist's couch pretty quick. I was a wreck. I cannot imagine what I'll do when I actually have to let them go off to college. That might break me.

At first I resented school. I wanted them home, wanted them to give me a purpose again, but I knew that was not the healthy way of dealing. So I did what I do when I can't deal: I ran.

I ran to make sense of who I was now and what I was supposed to do. I ran because of the pain of not having my kids with me all the time, of allowing someone else to take part in molding them. I ran to clear my mind and set my soul free.

Slowly, I learned to like having "me time" again. I had forgotten during the last six years what that even looked like. I could run, do errands, do yoga—do my husband—and be a better mom when the girls got home. Glen and I learned to enjoy cocktails with lunch and adult conversations again.

I found myself, which changed our dynamic as well—for the better. I love my kids dearly, miss them while they are at school, and still fret about their safety (darn anxiety), but I also love being alone and doing "me" for a couple hours a day. No pressure, no expectations, and no regrets.

"I'm selfish, impatient, and a little insecure. I make mistakes,
I am out of control, and at times hard to handle. But if you
can't handle me at my worst then you sure as hell don't
deserve me at my best."
–Marilyn Monroe

...

LULULEMON'S SEAWHEEZE HALF MARATHON

August 23, 2014

It had been seven weeks since I last competed a real deal race (tough mudder excluded because that was just raw and filthy fun), and in that time I had hosted a race and gotten down and dirty. Now Anna and I were returning to Vancouver for Lululemon's SeaWheeze Half Marathon, except this time I was going to get to experience the race for myself and not from the seat of a bike. Anna, on the other hand, had not had time to train for the race. She would be doing a little of what I had done last year, running a shorter race of her own jurisdiction, and hoping to see me at a few points.

I was not too worried about the race. In fact, I was rather calm about it, kind of a "what's meant to be will be" demeanor. It helped knowing how casual the race environment was, and with that in mind we woke up at 5 a.m. the day before the race to get in line for what would probably be the most stressful part of the weekend: the exclusive apparel store put on by Lululemon.

Believe it or not, this shopping experience was way more stressful than the impending race. Basically you get up at the crack of dawn, hair a mess, teeth barely brushed, to hurry to the line that was already a good hundred people deep. Then you wait until 8 a.m. when the doors open. Why do this, you ask?

This is limited-edition, one-of-a-kind, can't-find-anywhere-else, exclusive-to-the-race Lululemon gear, and those who know anything about me and Anna know we don't mess around when it comes to Lululemon. Having done this the year before, we had a system and had mapped out a plan. We would get in line, one of us would go to the Starbucks across the street for our first Green Tea Lemonade (we don't mess around when it comes to Starbucks either), and come back to hang until our drinks were gone. Then the other person would head back to Starbucks and get more.

We had to keep our spirits and caffeine intake up to get through the next few hours. Before too long it was 8 a.m., and we were in the first group ushered through the door.

Now picture, if you will, a large, high-ceilinged ballroom overlooking the mountains and the bay. (Stunning, no?) But then you look out in front of you, and hundreds of women (and a few straggling men) are grabbing everything they can in their size, running around like chickens with their heads cut off, and eventually finding a spot on the floor with all their garb, stripping down to try on the clothes. (I mean, there were bare asses everywhere.)

Sure, there are dressing rooms, but that would require waiting in line and wasting valuable time, so few people used them. Chaos is not even close to accurate to describe this; it is more like pandemonium mixed with havoc, fueled by hormones and greed.

I have a weird anxiety quirk when it comes to clothing. I am paranoid that someone is going to swoop in and grab what I want right before I can get it. There is a reason for this, and it stems back to high school. I had fallen in love with these jeans, and as any woman knows, finding a good pair of jeans is no small feat. I decided after awhile that I loved them so much that I should own another pair. I returned to the store only to learn they were sold out and had discontinued the style. I was devastated. To this day, anytime I like something, I buy it in bulk. A couple pairs, a couple different colors, whatever I need to make sure I don't miss out on something I love again.

So this ballroom was ramping up my anxiety in a big way. I was one of them, grabbing, hoarding, and analyzing the gear, fearing someone was going to take the last size of the one thing I wanted. Since there are limited quantities, when it is gone, it is gone forever. I would have popped a Xanax if I'd had one.

Needless to say, it was worth it, and Anna and I made it out alive with some great duds. We spent the rest of the day shopping, consuming more Starbucks, napping, and eventually eating the best Mexican food I have ever eaten. (In Canada! Who knew?) I later realized Mexican might not have been the best prerace dinner choice, but it tasted good going down.

The next morning we got ready for the race, grabbed our Starbucks (don't even ask how many GTLs we consumed in Canada), and headed to the starting line. I went into the race thinking it may not be my best, since it had been a long time since I had run a half, but I wanted to try to really enjoy the beauty that was about to surround me for the next thirteen miles. After all, we weren't that far from Snoqualmie, and we all know how much that race moved me.

Before I knew it we were off, running the streets of downtown Vancouver. We ran past the piers and Rogers Arena (where the Canucks play), and then headed down toward the water on one side of the bay. Having biked the course the year before, I knew we would soon happen upon those awesome drag queens. Anna was also hoping to see me at this point.

I saw the queens first, followed by Queen Anna herself, who waved and cheered as I went by her, up the hill, over a beautiful bridge, and down into another unique part of Vancouver. The course wound past Lululemon headquarters (kind of a mecca for us) and into a little neighborhood, where we turned around and headed back.

Back across the bridge and into the woods, veering around a corner, there we were, on the much-anticipated "Seawall" of Vancouver. The Seawall is a stone wall constructed all around Stanley Park, with a path separating the park from the bays and inlets. It is far and away one of the coolest running paths I have ever been on. You are running with a huge forest-like park on one side, the water in the bay on the other, and mountains and hills all around you. It's quite a sight to behold.

It was out along this path, with nothing but nature surrounding me, that I got lost in thought. Beauty enclosed me, God's creation everywhere. I had been so busy trying to outrun my anxiety that I had forgotten to slow down and actually enjoy running. I wanted this race to be different. I wanted to stop and smell the roses. (Without actually stopping, of course. I am too type A for that.)

I tried to take it in, slow down, pray, and let the run consume me. Anna had found me on the Seawall and kept up with me for a short time; somehow on my "relax-and-enjoy-it" run I was managing to keep a pretty good clip. We were soon out of the Seawall and only had one mile remaining.

With that last mile to go I saw her again, just for a second, as she cheered me on and headed toward the finish. Rounding that last turn, I felt amazing—not tired, not spent, just pure exhilaration. I had run an amazing race, and had a chance to take it in as well.

I crossed the finish line at 1:50:27, which was way better than I had ever imagined going into the race. After some Starbucks (duh), a nap, and a shower (yes, in that order), we ventured back to our favorite Mexican restaurant for a celebratory dinner (since I had managed to keep the grub from the night before in during the race). We cheers'd to finishing the 2014 race season and to what would come when we returned to Vancouver in the New Year. We signed up immediately for the next year's race, which would sell out in less than twenty minutes. (Talk about anxiety.)

I would say that it is a tradition for us to go now, but the hubby says nothing is a tradition until you do it for three years in a row. So after we hit America's top hat in 2015, Vancouver will officially be my favorite girls' trip tradition.

"If you aren't going to say exactly how and what you feel,
you might as well not say anything at all."
–Johnny Cash

...

MONSTER DASH 5K

October 25, 2014

To say that a lot happened since I last lined up to start the Lululemon race would be an understatement, and that was only two months ago. I had taken on a job, and Glen was out a knee (Remember when I had hoped he would get through his bucket list item with his knee intact... no luck).

First things first. Glen went under the knife just a few days after the season was done to have his knee cleaned out. I had this same procedure done twice (yes, it is amazing that I can still run), once in 2001 and again in 2006. I gave him fair warning about how sick I got during the procedure and how awful the recovery was.

As with any injury, time seems to be the enemy. Your body never heals as fast as you want or as easily as you hope. Most of the time other things come up and prevent you from getting right back at it. This was the case with my two knee surgeries. I was sick from the anesthesia, then the stim at rehab almost made me pass out; the monotonous small movements bored me to death. It is amazing I made it through (first world problems I know).

I admit I have been pretty lucky in the injury department as it pertains to running. Other than my post-marathon debacle, I have only had a few bumps and bruises; my issues seem to be more mental than physical.

I was preparing for the worst when I met Glen in the postsurgical room. Instead he was all smiles and asked me if we could stop at Chipotle on the way home. I figured he must still be coming down from the pain meds, but he was serious. When we pit-stopped on the way home so he could down a burrito, I tried to conceal my resentment.

While Glen was on the mend—did I mention he was up and walking the same day? Show-off!—I was being courted. I arrived home from Vancouver to an email from Jay Corn, editor at *RedCurrent*, a blog with a mission to tell the stories of people involved in various events throughout the Twin Cities.

I had spoken with Jay earlier in the month about Fifteen's 5k, and he had noticed my blog at the bottom of my email. He had been reading it and apparently liked what he read, as his email was part thank-you for Fifteen's 5k information and part job offer.

He wanted me to be a contributing writer. Me, with no experience or formal writing training, only the prerequisite English and writing courses needed for my elementary education degree. Me, who used tons of ellipses. ("Thinking dots," Jay called them.) I wrote the way I heard the wording in my head rather than the way you were supposed to. But he wanted me. I was humbled.

I was not sure what I could offer, but Jay felt I could offer a lot, and so after a coffee meeting with Jay and Pete (*RedCurrent*'s creator), I was a bona fide writer. Now this stay-at-home mom, baseball wife, and crazy runner could add professional writer to her résumé.

I was so honored they wanted to take a chance on me, and I did not want to disappoint. I hit the ground running, as I usually do. I wrote my first piece about the Fifteen's 5k experience, followed by my Minnesota State Fair dilemma. I absolutely love the state fair, but our state fair visit is different than that of most, because we have to do it gluten-free and dairy-free. Surprisingly, there are still plenty of delicious things to eat. It is part of what makes the Minnesota State Fair so great. I wanted to give others who are doing the same thing ideas on how to enjoy the Great Minnesota Get-Together while adhering to dietary restrictions. (Captivating subject, I know, but I still felt good about it.)

It was nice to be doing something positive and to be appreciated for something you never knew was in you. I wanted to do something groundbreaking with this opportunity, though I wasn't sure what that was yet. I would soon figure it out.

One day, after running an idea by Jay, I sat down at my computer to come clean, bare the truth, and let the world in on my secret.

I have always been honest with my family and friends about my struggles with anxiety, and I hoped by sharing my truth I would help others. I have never understood the stigma around mental illness or why people feel ashamed, like they have to hide something they can't control. My experience with anxiety led me to write a piece for *RedCurrent* titled "You Are Not Alone: Starting a Conversation about Mental Illness."

I wanted to come clean. I wanted to be able to leave my medicine bottle out and not feel ashamed. I wanted others to see the wife of a Twins player be brutally honest. I wanted everyone to be honest about who they are.

The words came as easily as I could imagine, almost like the story had been in my head all along, just waiting to come out. I wrote about how I had found out about my diagnosis, how I see a therapist, that I am on meds, how much running helps, and most importantly, that I am not humiliated.

I wanted people to know that there is nothing to hide; you are who you are, and you are amazing and you are a miracle. I shared my inner demons in order to help others do the same.

Even as I finished the piece and was ready to send it to my editor I had a moment of panic. What would people think of me now? Would they think I am crazy? Would they tiptoe around me? Did I want to admit this to the world? Would they judge me?

But it was those very thoughts that had led me to write the piece to begin with. I no longer wanted others to tell me what "normal" looked like, and with a pit in my stomach I pressed Send and waited to see what the world would do with my admission.

What transpired out of my honesty was far more than Jay, Pete, or I could have imagined.

The post garnered a ton of traffic and led to me doing news segments, radio, and more interviews about my blog. The response was so overwhelmingly positive it blew me away. I had worried what people would think of me—would they call me crazy, mentally ill, different?—but instead they called me brave, authentic, inspirational, and honest. I was so moved by the comments and emails from people thanking me for shedding light on a dark subject. I received emails asking me to emcee events and lead walks for mental illness. People were offering me a chance to be the face of this disorder, and while I was a little nervous, I was excited to strip away the preconceived notions of what mental illness looks like.

My honesty and transparency had forced the conversation to the forefront. If a Twins wife could tell her story to the world, then people felt they could at least tell their friends.

While the post was great for *RedCurrent*, and positive and therapeutic for me, I was most concerned as to whether my article helped others talk about their anxiety, come forward, and not be afraid; whether it helped them tell others, seek treatment, and not live in fear or in pain.

My therapist told me she actually had someone come in and tell her they had seen a Twins wife share her story on the news, and that I had made them realize that if I could be that brave, so could they. My therapist just smiled, knowing it was me, and knowing I had made a difference, something I never would have been able to do years ago before I sought help myself.

One note about my therapist. I have mentioned how amazing she is and the power I feel after leaving her office, but I need to clarify that I was not always this lucky. I have had my fair share of bad therapists, the ones that, in the end, do more damage than good. But I want to emphasize that just because the first person you see may not be "your person," you need to keep looking. You will find that person, and when you do, you will be forever grateful. What works for one person may not for another. I love my therapist, but that doesn't mean she is right for you, and that is ok as long as you find the person that is.

I saw my first therapist in junior high after my grandfather passed away. We were close, it was sudden, and I couldn't deal, so my parents had me see someone. In retrospect I realize this was really proactive for my mom, who wouldn't even talk about her anxiety, much less see someone for it. I wish she would, but I am glad that she at least did it for me. Unfortunately, this guy really had no profound effect on me whatsoever. I don't recall feeling any better after the few times that I saw him, and so I stopped going and was left in the lurch dealing with all these emotions on my own.

My visits with the second therapist I saw ended with a similar result. I began seeing her in high school after my longtime boyfriend and I had broken up, when I thought the world was going to end.

Remember that first heartbreak experience? It is the absolute worst, and you think you will never get past it. Of course you do, and it makes you stronger, but in the moment you are sure this is going to be the end of you. I was hormonal, devastated, and broken. I threatened to leave my parents' house and move in with my grandmother because they just did not understand. I even wrote them a note, saying it would be "better this way." I mean, really?

Remember when I told you I put my parents through a hormonal ringer? This is the kind of crap I was talking about. What a high-school-girl thing to say and do. I was a hot mess. They, of course, did not let me go to my grandma's, and instead had me see a therapist. She and I just did not jive, and in the end my heart healed on its own, as it always does with time.

So when the idea of seeing someone was again brought to the forefront, I was skeptical. Lucky for me, my uncle had seen Dr. D (my therapist) after his divorce and really loved working with her, so I made the call. To my surprise, I loved her too. She has been such an amazing and invigorating part of my life ever since. I am not sure where I would be today without our connection.

My advice in all of this is if you are going to see someone (and I think the entire world would be a better place if everyone did), ask around and get some referrals. As is true in any profession, some therapists are awesome and some are not. You need to find the one that jives with you. It may not be the first person you see, or the second, or even the third, but you need to keep trying until you find the one, because once you do, it is so worth it. Trust me.

Back to the post. It was good. Heck, it was great. I had done something worthwhile with my writing. I was not just writing fluff pieces, and I had now done something real and beneficial. The story of me, my struggle, what helped, and what didn't wasn't over in a two-part blog series; I knew I had much more to say. So after the hoopla around the story died down and September became October, I flirted with the idea of writing a book.

There you have it. By the time we were about to start the Monster Dash 5k on October 25, a lot had changed. Anna and I ran with the kiddos again, but instead of crayons we had two lady cops, an army man, and Olaf from *Frozen*. We were quite the crew.

We also had with us another girlfriend of mine, Nicole, and her daughter, Tessa. This was another ploy to get my kids to like running. I figured if I kept adding people, I would add to the fun, and maybe, just maybe, they would look forward to it.

Handfuls of candy, lots of smiles, and 3.1 miles later, we could cross this year's Monster Dash 5k off the list. I am proud to say that the girls ran more of the race than they had the year before. I have no idea about our time—the kids wouldn't care anyway—and as far as I was concerned, it was a victory: we all finished and were still smiling after.

"Anything's possible if you've got enough nerve."
–J. K. Rowling

...

HOOTERS TO HOOTERS HALF MARATHON

March 1, 2015

Don't you love how I just conveniently skip over the dreaded Minnesota winters? I spent this one just like I did the last, and all the others before that: on the treadmill watching my "stories," with the exception of one odd day at the end of January where it was 50 degrees. I actually ventured my hibernating butt outside and hit the pavement, and even ran through some snow.

I sometimes think I should come up with a digital race that is run on the treadmill in the wintertime. I, for one, need a way to stay motivated as the snow falls and the treadmill miles rise. I do still run in the nastiness of the Minnesota winter, but as you know, it is from the comfort of my warm 65-degree basement with my oscillating fan blowing on me. Oh, the fan ... a key part of my treadmill miles that brings me back to my childhood. The hot nights in the cabin lying on your bed with slightly sunburned skin in nothing but your underwear, trying desperately not to shift because the slightest movement makes you feel even hotter in that non-air-conditioned room. I would lie there and pray that I could actually fall asleep while waiting for that amazing breeze as the fan slowly glided over me, only to turn away and leave me waiting again. Being up at the cabin brought some of my greatest and most calming memories to date, so at times when I need to relax and take a deep breath, I remember the cabin and my love affair with the fan.

In the dead of winter, even though I can't feel the pavement under my feet, I am still diligent, still keep my endurance up. I try at all times to train as though I have a half marathon coming up. I keep myself in good enough shape to bang out 13.1 miles at the drop of a hat, and never want to be far from that point physically; I always want to keep up with how far I have come. If you let yourself fall too far from that, it is hard to come back.

I did get a break from the treadmill when we mixed in a trip to Costa Rica, where I got a chance to hit the pavement again—extremely hot and humid pavement, but pavement nonetheless.

Every year Nike takes some of its best baseball players on an all-expenses-paid trip to a fun location as a thank-you for being a Nike athlete. We had never been invited on the trip before, but Glen and I had heard great things from friends. We were excited, and would spend the next week hanging out with some of the most fun people I have ever met. We spent the week zip-lining, snorkeling, sailing on a catamaran, paddle boarding, running, hiking, drinking, eating, laughing, and letting loose.

It was hot as balls there. It felt like running on the edge of hell, yet you were surrounded by a heavenly landscape. The humidity was intense, and the hills were killer. The landscape and crystal-teal ocean views were breathtaking, but the heat was already taking my breath away. Running that close to the equator and on such tough terrain made for some of the hardest runs I had ever done. For as hard as it was, it was that beautiful and rewarding too. God's creation is so incredible if you take the time to think about the amazing places where only your feet can take you. I did that in Costa Rica; I was soaking it in under my sweat-drenched tee.

I got to know some of the great people who work for Nike, and they may have even convinced me to run Hood to Coast with them in the near future. Hood to Coast is a twelve-person, 195-mile event that starts at Mount Hood in Portland, Oregon, and ends on the beach in Seaside, Oregon. Once your team starts the race, you don't stop. Teams run day and night in shifts of about six to seven miles, and you sleep in the van when you can. By the end, each person has run about twenty-one miles.

The only catch is I'd have to do the race in Nike shoes, which I hadn't run in since high school. I made a mental note to order some Nikes when I got home from Costa Rica. High school flashbacks, here I come.

Once back in Minnesota and back on the treadmill, we made a huge family decision that had quite an effect on my anxiety and the number of treadmill miles I booked that off-season.

I wanted my kids to have a dog. I think it is good for them, but I was scared. Scared of new responsibility, scared of the unknown (Anxiety 101). I was not going to let my fear prevent my kids from having something I thought they needed.

In August my brother Luke had gotten a mini goldendoodle, Yoshi, and the kids had fallen in love with him. I, too, fell in love with his personality. So we found a trainer who would take the puppy from the breeder and lay the groundwork. This was the only way I was going to be able to do this with my anxiety. I needed to get rid of some of the unknowns.

I also started seeing my therapist more through the winter months to talk about it, and with a plan in place, and unbeknownst to the girls, we picked a goldendoodle puppy out via Skype from the breeder in Indiana. At eight weeks he was sent by plane to the trainer in Connecticut for six weeks before he came to us.

He was a bona fide traveler before he even got to his forever home.

We had wanted to give him to the girls as a Christmas present, but because the timing didn't work out, he landed in Minnesota on Black Friday. Their jaws dropped, and they looked at me saying, "Whose puppy is that? Is it ours?"

They couldn't believe it when we nodded yes, and I got two of the biggest hugs I have ever received. After a few days on Xanax, I was able to finally allow myself to let the dog in my heart and let the fear go. Anxiety told me I couldn't, but I fought back and did it anyway.

I had never taken or even been prescribed Xanax before we got Harry Potter, but after talking with my therapist about the level of anxiety I was feeling before he even arrived, it was apparent to her that I needed something to get me through the first few days with him, the ones where anxiety would tell me I couldn't do this, that he needed to go.

I was skeptical as to whether this little pill could alter my feelings so quickly. I was sure this was not going to work and that I would be spending the first few days with him experiencing a mild panic attack. The last time we had tried to get a dog I cried every day he was with us; I would try not to be home to look at him, and he consumed my every thought. I couldn't sleep, eat, or breathe. My chest hurt, and I lost five pounds in a week—and I am not a big person. The horrible part was that the dog was a good boy, was a normal cute puppy, but it was me that couldn't handle it. I had no reason not to love the dog. By the end of the week the dog was gone and so was my panic attack. I was deathly afraid the same thing would happen with Harry Potter, and I couldn't do that to my kids.

Xanax is a powerful drug and can be addictive. It should only be used as directed, and in times when it is truly needed. That being said, it is an amazing little pill. I was floored with the level of calm and ease it brought to my life at a time when I was ready for a full-out panic attack. I am not sure that Harry Potter would still be living with us had it not been for the Xanax. I am happy to say that after four days I stopped taking it, and haven't needed it since. I have it in my purse in case a situation arises and am glad to know it is there, but I hope I never need it again.

Harry Potter has been such a joy to both of the girls, and has brought so much love to their lives. They dote on him, carry him around, and love the daylights out of him. He is so good to them and puts up with everything they put him through. He is an incredibly good dog, and as much as I hate to admit it, I am in love with him too (as much as I hate to concede it being the self admitted "girl who is indifferent on dogs"). He has truly rounded out our family—anxiety be damned.

Now that I have caught you up on our treadmill-filled months of winter, let's come back to March 1, 2015, when we were in Fort Myers for spring training. We were spending the weekend with some of the greatest runners I know: Jeff, Bekah, Travis (our amazing manual therapist), and his better half, Becky. One of them even won the Hooters to Hooters Half Marathon that we all ran.

These are the runners that I am in awe of. Just being around them gives you a contact high and makes you want to run more. They are fast, smooth, and effortless, and clearly love to run. I like to think that I love to run, that it is such a big part of me, but being around them makes me feel like I am more of a jogger than a runner. These are the "real runners," the ones from whom the name stems.

While we did spend some of the weekend getting worked on by Travis, most of the time was spent eating great grub, drinking good cocktails, engaging in awesome conversation, and running with some of the best pals a girl could ask for.

We headed out on our first group run Friday morning. We lasted as a five-some for about a half mile before the boys promptly left us in the dust, which, of course, was to be expected. Then it was just the girls for the next four miles before Becky veered off and left Bekah and me to run another three alone. It reminded me how much I missed running with Bekah.

A couple of years ago, before my recurrent sinus infections, her wedding, Mill City Running, and crazy kid activities, we used to meet weekly and run. Though she was faster than me, she always hung back and visited as we trekked those two loops around Cleary Lake.

I thoroughly enjoyed revisiting those times while she was in Florida. Bekah was, after all, my very first running partner.

The highlight of the weekend was the Hooters to Hooters Half Marathon we had all registered to run. We got up at the butt crack of dawn, donned our Mill City gear, fueled up, and piled in the van for what we were sure would be an interesting race. Jeff hoped to win it—yes, the whole darn thing. Can you imagine what it must be like to think "Oh, maybe I'll try to win this," and actually be able to do it? I am just thrilled to not die along the way, and he was going to try to be the very first one across the finish line.

We got to the race, registered, and Jeff promptly went his separate way to mentally and physically prepare for what lay ahead. The rest of us walked around and people watched. (Believe me, there was some good people watching.)

Before long it was go-time. The race started late (apparently this was normal), and as they said *Go!* Jeff and the faster ones took off as Bekah and Travis and I hung back. Becky and Bekah were going to be doing the half as a relay, so Becky was waiting at the 6.5-mile mark to take Bekah's bib. We visited the first two miles, and while I thought we were moving at a pretty fast clip (8:10 per mile), I could tell Bekah and Travis were itching to go, so I let them free after mile 2.

After that I was on my own, just the Fort Myers landscape and me. The course was pretty flat 90 percent of the time, except for the two miles of bridge over the water that was a pretty steep hill up and down. I was ready for the change of terrain, but afterward it hit me hard.

The bridge occurred during miles 7 through 9, and the following mile (9 to 10) made me feel like I had hit a wall. My legs were shot from the hill, and it was hot and humid as all get-out. I kept going, just one foot in front of the other, and then at mile 11 I saw Becky not too far ahead of me so I picked up my pace. She was the magical energy boost that I needed. I caught her right before 11.75 miles and chatted for a minute before passing her, which, I will admit, felt good. (Sorry, Becky.)

I mixed in a quick bathroom stop, and before I knew it I was on the last mile. It was scorching, sticky, and hard, but when I saw Travis near the finish and gave him our little dance move, I was feeling like I could do this. Then I saw Jeff, and knowing how hard he ran made me kick it into high gear. I sprinted past Bekah, so fast she couldn't even get a photo of me, and I crossed the finish line looking like a badass. I even beat some old guy across the line . . . success!

I may have gone a little too fast at the end, because I felt like I was going to throw up after. I am not sure if it was the race, the scorching Florida heat, or the smell of the wings that were being consumed nearby, but it took everything in me not to toss my cookies. So, if you are keeping track, the score is: tossing cookies–0, Alisha–3.

My time, 1:53:33, placed me at 171 out of 812 people. Not my best, but I'll take it. Plus, we all know I had to let Jeff win or it would have killed his ego.

Race season 2015 had officially kicked off.

"We are all broken; that's how the light gets in."
-Ernest Hemingway

...

GOLDY'S 10 MILE RACE

April 11, 2015

Here we are, having come full circle, back to Hemingway and to the very first race I ever ran, Goldy's 10 Mile. I hate to admit it, but I actually was not able to run this race. I had planned on it, trained for it, and paid for it, but God had other plans. Instead, I was home alone with the kids, and Addie was up all night with a 103-degree fever and a wheezing cough that turned out to be influenza. Needless to say, when 6:30 a.m. rolled around there was no way I was leaving my baby to run. I was bummed, but such is life. I love this race and hope to run it again next year with Annie by my side. I will forever think of the University of Minnesota as a second home, and running through it every year makes me feel safe.

It is crazy to think that I have come full circle my fifth year as a runner. When one becomes a runner something changes. Not immediately, but over time. You start to see things differently, feel things in other ways, and grow in ways you didn't even know you needed to.

Running changes you in ways you didn't even know were possible. For me, running made a dramatic difference in my life. How so?

Well, I learned that speeding up can help you slow down.

I learned this the hard way. By now you know all too well about my struggles with anxiety. I tried therapy and medication, and both helped significantly, but running plays one of the biggest roles in my anxiety release.

I found out that the harder, faster, longer, and more frequently I run, the easier it is to release the adrenaline buildup from the anxiety, and I am able to level myself out more.

Running is a natural and easy way to slow my thoughts down, process them, and help me function at a more even level. It helps align my thoughts and calm my fears.

I learned that holding on can help you let go.

Our everyday responsibilities can get the best of us. The to-do lists that never end, the constant demands. How do you get away from it all? How do you make time for you?

For me, setting a goal or signing up for a race and holding steadfast to the training helps me let go of all the other things I "should" be doing and focus on what I "need" to do for me.

We so often put ourselves on the back burner and start this vicious cycle where we wear ourselves down and lose sight of who we are. Make a goal and stay true to you. You deserve it.

I learned that going alone is good for the soul.

I love my running partner. Let's just put that out there. She holds me accountable, and she gives me a reason to look forward to running.

That being said, there is something about being out there on the open road alone. I am a mother of two girls whom I love dearly, but there are times when the only "me" time I get is when I am out on a run.

Even when there is a hard day or I don't want to run, I try to remember that the run is necessary for me to be a better mom, wife, daughter, sister, and friend. So I lace up and head out the door.

I learned that accepting help is not admitting defeat.

This was a tough one for me. I am a type A perfectionist, and stubborn. I tend to think there is nothing I can't do on my own, or do better on my own. Admitting failure or inadequacy is painful for me—I mean gut-wrenching.

So when I decided to finally cross "running a marathon" off my bucket list it pained me to ask for help training . . . but I knew I needed the help of a professional.

Lucky for me I did not have to look far. Bekah was my best asset.

I highly recommend getting a coach if you can. If not, be active in the running community. Ask other runners for their experiences, stories, advice, and mantras. Don't be afraid; runners are generally nice people.

I learned that you can, in fact, run away from your problems.

I feel all this pent-up stress and needed to get away. In those moments the very best thing to do is lace up and get out.

You will be amazed at how much more you can align your thoughts and feelings after that run. Something happens out there on the road, on your own. It all calms down, falls apart, and yet all comes together. Life just doesn't feel as scary after your run. You come back refreshed and adjusted.

Of course, these are all just my experiences, but I feel like most of them are a common thread in the running community. I run because, somehow, completely exhausting myself is the most relaxing part of my day.

I never thought that one sport could change my entire outlook on life until I became a runner. Listen, that is saying a lot, because I am a baseball wife, and believe you me, that sport changes our lives in countless ways.

It not only pays the bills but dictates our day-to-day schedules and controls our lives. Running, on the other hand, is different. I control it, and therefore it becomes a release instead of a restraint.

It is funny how the lessons of running parallel the lessons of our lives:

Preparation is key. Just like in life, if you don't prepare for a race, you won't succeed. If you're going to take the ACT, study up. If you're going to hook a client, make sure that PowerPoint kicks ass. If you want to go from the couch to a 5k, consult an app. If you want to run a marathon, get a coach. You know what I am getting at.

Most things in life have a better outcome when you go in prepared. Don't go on a long run without an energy or water supply. Don't try to run in those old gym shoes from high school. Don't sign up for a marathon a month before it starts with little to no training. (This one has an exception: see "Sharktrek.")

Ok, this is not always true. There are times when things go your way with little to no preparation, and times that you work so hard and things still fall apart.

This happens in running too, even to the best of us. You set out on that long run and no matter what you do, you just can't get into it; you are off.

On the other hand, you drank that entire bottle of wine the night before, fully expecting a terrible run the next day, and instead you PR. I am not saying that you can't be the recipient of some blind luck, but for the most part it is better to have your ducks in a row.

I learned that I get by with a little help from my friends.

Let's face it, there are times in your life that you never would have gotten through without your friends. The people who encourage, inspire, and love you no matter what. You know who they are and you know how much you need them.

There are people like that in running, too. Whether it is your trusty running partner, the friendly folks at the running store, or that person running next to you in a race, they are part of what keep you going (you were racing and they didn't even know it). These are your running friends; they help you laugh during those crappy races, and remind you that running can be fun.

I learned that you get out of it what you put into it.

I want you all to know that I am not an Oprah fan; in fact, I really don't care for her at all. However, Oprah ran a marathon, and let me say, if she can do it with the schedule she keeps, then anyone can, am I right?

As she was training she said, "Running is the greatest metaphor for life, because you get out of it what you put into it."

In life that is not always the case. You may want it to be—heck, all of us type A people really wish it were true—but it is not. Truthfully it is one of the most beautiful things about running, and maybe one of the reasons so many people love it. You really do get out of it what you put in. How many other things in life can you say that about?

I learned that time is of the essence.

In this extremely fast-paced world, everything needs to be done yesterday. You know what I am talking about; if you send someone a text or email and he or she doesn't get back to you in five minutes you begin to think they are mad at you. *What did I do? Why are they mad? Why haven't they gotten back to me?*

It can be so stressful to live in this world, one where we are constantly waiting to see those text dots appear.

Before I was a runner (a term I still hate to use—it implies I know what I am doing), I used to run up to two miles every once in a while to stay in shape. This was back when I still had an awesome metabolism and didn't need to exercise to stay thin. (Oh, the early twenties.)

Anyway, I will never forget the day I ran over four miles. I swear that is when the runner's high kicks in, that elusive, amazing feeling where running goes from a chore to an addiction. Trust me, go, get lost, go over four miles, and let time slip away as you discover what it feels like to love running, not loathe it.

I learned that not all who wander are lost.

I have always had a hard time with this one in the real world. Maybe because I am too type A to wander around without a plan, or maybe I just can't handle not having a schedule. Either way, though this concept is foreign in my life, it is not foreign in my running.

There is nothing better than going for a run and ending up somewhere you have never been. I love getting lost in the moment.

My life creeps into my running the same way that running creeps into my life. There is something so natural about it and yet so foreign. So much to explore and yet so much you already know about it.

Go ahead, get lost. Lace up your shoes and learn more about yourself.

I often think back to the beginning of my running journey and our baseball life; we were green and excited, naïve and overzealous. We were so young, thrust into this crazy world. We thought we were ready, but we had no idea what lay ahead.

Now here we are, ten years later (five years as a runner), older(ish), wiser, humbled, and clued in. We now know what it takes to make it in this game of baseball and out on the road running, and what the game and the road take from you in return. Glen and I came into this together, clueless and ignorant, and now we are on the other side—still together, stronger. What a difference a few years can make.

So what happens next? Where do my feet take me from here? Where does this leave my anxiety? My family?

My hope for Glen is that he gets to leave baseball on his terms (few do) and that the game doesn't force us out. I hope the fans continue to support and encourage him, and continue to be patient with him.

I hope he finds something that will make him happy once it is all said and done, maybe in the front office for the Twins. I want him to feel good about his place in the "civilian world," to feel wanted and useful. I want the media to use grace with him and allow mistakes to be just that, to focus on the good and let the bad days go.

I hope he grows in his faith and gets to enjoy moments with his family that he missed out on because of baseball. I hope someday he will go for a run with me.

My hope for my kids is they grow up with a godly heart, an open mind, a tolerant spirit, and a giving soul. I want them to be generous, kind, compassionate, thoughtful, passionate, and humble. I hope they know they are no different just because of who their dad is, and that no one person is above another. I hope they know that what someone says about you says more about them than it does about you. I hope they know they can do anything but not everything. I hope they find something that brings them as much joy as running has brought me. I hope they know they are loved no matter what, and that they never let success go to their head or failure go to their heart. I want them to know they are a miracle and that they are amazing.

And for me?

Well, there are a lot of things I hope for myself.

I hope I am the type of mother who has full hands and a full heart, and can give my kids roots and help them find their wings. I hope to have the type of marriage that grosses my kids out now and yet makes them want to get married someday.

I want to be the type of friend who is fiercely loyal and crazy fun. I want to learn to give myself grace when it comes to my anxiety and type A personality. I hope I run another marathon. (Don't tell Glen.) I hope I don't miss baseball when it is all said and done. I want to have no regrets. I hope I am someone my girls look up to. I hope I wake up with determination and go to bed with satisfaction. I hope my faith is bigger than my fear. I want to be truly comfortable in my own skin.

I hope that God continues to give strength to my steps so that no matter where I wind up, I can always run home.

4/9/11   Goldy's 10 mile   1:37:21
6/5/11   Minneapolis Half   2:02:42
8/6/11   Minnesota Half 1:56:45
8/21/11   13.1 Minneapolis 1:54:01
10/29/11   Monster Dash   1:44:12
12/4/11   Lululemon Hot Toddies Run
2/26/12   Disney Princess Half 1:44:03
4/14/12   Goldy's 10 mile   1:29:20
5/5/12   Snoqualmie Half   1:48:16
6/16/12   Grandma's Half 1:46:02
7/15/12   Color Run 5k
8/11/12   Gopher to Badger Half 1:46:20
9/1/12   Women Rock Half   1:51:58
10/7/12   Twin Cities 10 mile   1:18:57
10/14/12   San Fran Nike LLS Half 1:47:21
10/21/12   Monster Dash 10/5k 1:22:29
4/13/13   Goldy's 10 mile 1:27:46
6/1/13   Minneapolis Marathon   4:01:29
7/4/14   Red, White, and Boom Half 1:52:57
7/20/14   Tough Mudder
8/23/14   SeaWheeze Half   1:50:27
10/25/14   Monster Dash 5k
3/1/15   Hooters to Hooters Half   1:53:33
4/11/15   Goldy's 10 Mile   0:00

Fifteen's 5k Races
8/12/12
8/18/13
8/17/14
8/2/15

ACKNOWLEDGMENTS

This book would not have been possible without these amazing people in my life:

To my husband who loves me without restriction, trusts me without fear, wants me without demand, and accepts me for who I am. The most wonderful thing I ever decided to do was to share my life and heart with you.

To my daughters who love me with reckless abandon and make me feel like I am the best mom in the world. You are both such miracles and are so amazing. You challenge and inspire me. You give me purpose and peace. You are the best things that have ever been mine.

My parents, who always believe in me, encourage me, love me unconditionally, and instill a hope in me that makes me believe I can do anything.

Anna Biehn, the woman who was more excited than I was about this process and kept me going.

Bekah Metzdorf—she was one of my first inspirations to run.

Jenna Berg, the amazing lady who watched my girls so I could write.

Jay Corn, my *RedCurrent* editor, who believed in my voice and helped me draft my story.

The wonderful staff at North Loop Books, for dealing with my brand of crazy and helping make this book a reality.

John Courtright, for helping me at every turn and keeping my spirits up at all times.

My brother Luke, an amazing photographer and graphic designer, who always makes me look good.

To every runner out there who knows that running is not just a sport, but a way of life.

ABOUT THE AUTHOR

Alisha Perkins is mom to two girls, wife to three-time All-Star Minnesota Twins closer Glen Perkins, and owner to a dog, Harry Potter. She is a born and raised Minnesotan.

Alisha and Glen host Fifteen's 5k, an annual race held in Minneapolis that has benefitted the Cystic Fibrosis Foundation in the past and looks to expand charities in the future.

Alisha's writing has appeared in publications including *Women's Running, Huffington Post, Ultrarunning, Like the Wind, RedCurrent, Minneapolis Running, Most, Star Tribune, Girls with Sole, Twins* magazine, and others.

Running Home is her first book. You can visit her online at alishaperkins.com.